BLACK & DECKER®
HOME IMPROVEMENT LIBRARY™

Finishing
Basements
& Attics

Ideas & Projects for
Expanding Your Living Space

CREATIVE
PUBLISHING
international

MINNETONKA, MINNESOTA

www.howtobookstore.com

Contents

© Copyright 2000
Creative Publishing international, Inc.
5900 Green Oak Drive
Minnetonka, Minnesota 55343
1-800-328-3895
www.howtobookstore.com

Printed by R.R. Donnelly & Sons Co.
10 9 8 7 6 5 4 3 2 1

President/CEO: David D. Murphy
Vice President/Editor-in-Chief: Patricia K. Jacobsen
Vice President/Retail Sales & Marketing: Richard M. Miller

Executive Editor: Bryan Trandem
Creative Director: Tim Himsel
Managing Editor: Michelle Skudlarek
Editorial Director: Jerri Farris

Author & Lead Editor: Philip Schmidt
Editors: Nancy Baldrica, Ruth Taswell
Copy Editor: Jennifer Caliandro
Technical Photo Editor: Keith Thompson

Assistant Art Directors: Kari Johnston, Kevin Walton
Mac Designer: Kari Johnston
Illustrators: Jim Kehnie, Earl Slack, Rich Stromwall
Project Manager: Julie Caruso
Photo Researchers: Julie Caruso, Angela Hartwell
Studio Services Manager: Marcia Chambers
Studio Services Coordinator: Carol Osterhus
Photo Team Leader: Chuck Nields
Photographer: Tate Carlson
Scene Shop Carpenters: Scott Ashfield, Dan Widerski
Director of Production Services: Kim Gerber
Production Manager: Stasia Dorn

FINISHING BASEMENTS & ATTICS
Created by: The Editors of Creative Publishing international, Inc.,
in cooperation with Black & Decker. Black & Decker® is a trademark
of The Black & Decker Corporation and is used under license.

Library of Congress
Cataloging-in-Publication Data
Finishing basements & attics : ideas & projects
for expanding your living space.
p. cm. -- (Black & Decker home improvement library)
Includes index.

ISBN 0-86573-583-2 (softcover)
ISBN 0-86573-467-4 (hardcover)
1. Dwellings--Remodeling--Amateurs' manuals.
2. Basements--Remodeling--Amateurs' manuals.
I. Black & Decker Manufacturing Company (Towson, Md.) II. Series.
TH4816.35.F55 2000
643'.5--dc21
00-034565

Other titles from Creative Publishing international include:
New Everyday Home Repairs, Decorating With Paint & Wallcovering, Basic Wiring & Electrical Repairs, Advanced Home Wiring, Landscape Design & Construction, Bathroom Remodeling, Built-In Projects for the Home, Refinishing & Finishing Wood, Home Masonry Repairs & Projects, Building Porches & Patios, Flooring Projects & Techniques, Advanced Home Plumbing, Remodeling Kitchens, Stonework & Masonry Projects, Carpentry: Remodeling, Carpentry: Tools•Walls•Shelves•Doors, Great Decks, Building Decks, Advanced Deck Building, The Complete Guide to Home Plumbing, The Complete Guide to Home Wiring, The Complete Guide to Decks, The Complete Guide to Painting & Decorating, The Complete Guide to Creative Landscapes, The Complete Guide to Home Masonry, The Complete Photo Guide to Home Repair

Jeff Krueger©

Introduction

Finishing your basement or attic is the easiest way to add living space to your home. With the basic structure already in place, there's little heavy construction or outdoor work required, and the project shouldn't disrupt your daily life the way an addition would. Best of all, the potential square footage to be gained is significant. All of this means that finishing those unused spaces is a realistic and worthwhile do-it-yourself project.

This book can guide you through the entire finishing project. It's divided into seven sections that represent the major stages of finishing unused spaces, including the most important step of all: planning. In successful basement and attic conversions, it takes careful planning to fit together the many elements (ductwork, plumbing, structural members, walls, etc.) while maximizing living space. But in order to create a complete plan, you'll need to determine everything that's going into the project—from the under-floor drain pipes to the window trim—and not all projects follow the same construction sequence. Therefore, it's a good idea to read through this book entirely before you begin construction.

Part of your planning will be to determine how much of the work you'll do yourself and how much you'll hire professionals to do. For the most part, finishing an attic or basement can be an all-season project, giving you much greater flexibility than you would have when building an addition. Although attic and basement conversions are good do-it-yourself projects, few homeowners have the tools and skills required to complete all of the tasks involved. Many hire professionals to help with the planning and design, as well as the physical work.

Regardless of who does what work, you'll need to get building permits for your project—for several reasons. First, it's the law. Getting caught without permits will result in fines from the city and possibly trouble with your insurance company. And work done without a permit can cause complications if you try to sell your house. Secondly, because it's the law, not having permits may make it difficult to find good contractors to work on your project (they can lose their licenses). Third, and most important, having permits means all your work will be inspected by building inspectors to make sure it meets local building code requirements. Unless you've worked as an electrician, plumber, carpenter, and engineer, you probably won't know all the details that apply to your project—and neither this nor any other book can tell you everything. Building inspections will ensure your work is safe for you and your family.

As a final note, good luck. Finishing a basement or attic can be fun at times and challenging at others, but the results are always rewarding.

Ideas

Like all big remodeling projects, finishing an attic or basement involves a series of phases—there's budgeting, planning, and construction, to name a few. But perhaps the most enjoyable phase of all is the *ideas* phase. This is when you look at an unfinished space—the bare concrete, the framing filled with insulation—and think of all the things it could become. One of the best ways to generate ideas is to look at other people's homes to see how they've transformed their unused areas into comfortable rooms. This section shows you some of the most popular uses of basement and attic spaces, and it discusses some general planning issues for the different types of rooms, to help you make the most of your new living space.

If you're like most people, there's something driving the decision to undertake this project. Perhaps your parents are moving in and you'd like them to have personal quarters that offer privacy and independence, or maybe you're planning to work at home and need a dedicated office space. Even if the existing rooms in your house meet your everyday needs, remodeling allows you to create the rooms you've always wanted. Whatever your motivation, considering a wide variety of ideas will eventually help create a reality that reflects your personality and the way you live.

From a design standpoint, one of the advantages of basement or attic space is that it is away from the ordinary flow of traffic through the house (and can't be seen as you walk through the front door). This allows you to create more private rooms that won't be disturbed by guests and everyday household activity. On the other hand, you can make the basement or attic the center of activity—add a new hang-out place for your teenagers or a playroom for younger kids, for example. The separation between floors also gives you greater freedom when decorating the rooms, allowing you to choose styles that depart from the overall decorating scheme of the main floors of the house.

Home Office

Whether it's primarily used for running a business or paying personal bills, a home office is a more productive setting if it's separated from everyday household traffic and noise. Attics and basements offer seclusion from family activity and, often, plenty of space. But to create a home office that's quiet and practical as well as inviting, consider the inherent advantages and disadvantages of an attic or basement space.

Attic offices are often visually appealing rooms. Sloped ceilings, triangular walls, and charming nooks make for interesting work areas. And well-placed windows or skylights can provide tree-top views that brighten the space. Kneewalls in attics are just the right height (typically 5 ft. tall) for most office furniture, and the spaces behind kneewalls can be used for storing files and supplies. The remote location of an attic office, however, makes access a primary concern. If you'll be meeting with clients, for example, consider adding an exterior stairway leading to a separate entrance to the office. Also, make sure your office will remain comfortable throughout the day. Use blinds on skylights and windows to reduce heat and glare from direct sunlight, and install an air conditioner or provide central-air

Photo courtesy of Kraftmaid Cabinetry

service to keep the room cool and well-ventilated.

In a basement, the wide-open space is ideal for creating a large, formal office, but a quiet corner can be perfect for a small work station. Walkout basements are especially suitable for offices that receive visitors and clients, because they have their own outside entrances. You can add signage or landscape around the entrance to give it a professional appearance. But be sure to check the zoning requirements in your area regarding public office space.

Keep in mind that basement offices need plenty of lighting. An office that's too dark will be unappealing—to you and to clients. If possible, plan your office around an existing window, or add a window for more natural light. If the office has no windows, use abundant ambient lighting to give the room a general warmth.

Planning a basement or attic office that works for you involves many factors, including determining the best layout for your needs, ensuring comfort over long hours of work, and providing the necessary hookups for your equipment. Turn to pages 10-11 for help with some of these major planning issues.

Christian Korab©

(above) A work surface and some built-in cabinets may be all you need for a compact corner office.

(left) This spacious office includes multiple work areas to accommodate a variety of tasks.

(opposite) Custom features help make the most of this unique attic space. A divider unit follows the ceiling slope, and custom windows offer expansive views.

Karen Melvin©

Wall Layout

File Cabinet 20" × 15"

Desk 24" × 60"

Bookshelf 12" × 24"

Chair 18" × 18"

L-shaped Layout

File Cabinet 20" × 15"

Desk 24" × 60"

Chair 18" × 18"

Table 24" × 60"

Parallel Layout

Desk 24" × 54"

File Cabinet 20" × 15"

Chair 18" × 18"

Credenza 15" × 60"

Bookshelf 12" × 24"

U-shaped Layout

File Cabinet 20" × 15"

Desk 24" × 54"

Chair 24" × 24"

Credenza 18" × 72"

Bookshelf 12" × 48"

OFFICE LAYOUTS

These typical office layouts can help you find a configuration that will work for your given space. To help with your planning, think about the tasks you do most often and how much storage space you'll need for commonly used materials. Approximate sizes are given for each typical office element.

Wall Layout. With this simple layout, the desk and storage units are aligned along one wall. Although this is a good choice for offices with limited space, it is less efficient than other arrangements, because the elements are not always within easy reach.

L-shaped Layout. This configuration is the most effective for a corner. You can also use it to divide a space, by placing one leg of the "L" against a wall

and letting the other leg project out into the room. The L shape gives you fairly easy access to a large work surface.

Parallel Layout. In this arrangement, there are two desks or tables set a few feet apart from each other with a chair in between. A parallel layout makes it easy to separate your work by task; for example, you can set your computer on one surface and place your files and phone on the other.

U-shaped Layout. This layout creates the most efficient work area, because all of the elements are within easy reach. By adding a chair on the outside of one of the work surfaces, you can create a small conference area.

ERGONOMICS

To minimize discomfort and fatigue, include ergonomic design in your office plan. For starters, chairs and desktops should fit your body type and size. Select a chair that's fully adjustable, so you can set the height, back, seat, and arms exactly where you want them. Your primary work surfaces should be at least 24" wide and stand between 28" and 30" from the floor, with a leg clearance underneath of at least 25". Also make sure there's at least 34" of space between your work surfaces and any opposing walls (inset). The position of computer equipment is crucial to comfort. Your keyboard should be slightly lower than your elbows as you type (typically 25" to 29" above the floor). To avoid eye and neck strain, position your monitor at or below eye level.

WIRING

It's a good idea to have access to one or more new circuits that serve only your home office equipment. This will reduce the chances of downtimes caused by circuit overloads. To determine how much power is needed for your equipment, add up the amperage (amps) drawn by all of the pieces. The amps should be listed on the back of each device. The total number of amps used on one circuit should not exceed 80% of the circuit's rating. Install enough receptacles to accommodate the devices you currently have, as well as a few extras for equipment you may need in the future.

Also make sure you have all the communications wiring you'll need—for Internet access, fax machines, business and personal phone lines, etc. As with the electrical outlets, including extra wiring and jacks now may be far more convenient and cost effective than adding them later.

Family Room

Adding a family room to your attic or basement gives you the opportunity to include features that your home currently doesn't have. If your current living space is relatively formal, you may want to plan your new room for more casual activity, or vice versa. Or perhaps you'd like a room that can accommodate diverse pastimes—a place where you can be with your family while you work on a hobby, for example.

Many people expand into their attics or basements to accommodate a maturing family. And as children grow into their teen years, they often prefer to "hang out" in a space of their own, rather than the traditional family room. A space for kids should cater to their favorite household pastimes. For those who enjoy long sessions on the Internet, a dedicated computer center would be a popular spot, and an entertainment center is great for young music and movie fans. Whatever amenities you include, creating a room for your children might be more fun if you let them contribute to the design.

If you're planning a large family room, consider designing the space around a focal point, such as a built-in unit or even a large television. An attractive focal point helps define a comfortable seating arrangement that draws people together in a large space.

Balthazar Korab©

Another option is a family room that's versatile, accommodating quiet reading one day and a slumber party the next. If this is your goal, plan the room so that the furnishings can easily be rearranged. Also include extra electrical receptacles and phone and cable TV jacks for greater flexibility.

As for features, nothing makes a family room more cozy than a fireplace. While a traditional masonry fireplace is impractical for most remodels, installing a gas fireplace with direct venting is within the ability and budget of most do-it-yourselfers (see pages 150-156). A wet bar is another great addition to a new family room. A full-service wet bar—with a refrigerator/freezer, a microwave, and plenty of storage, can accommodate all types of entertaining (see pages 135-141).

Christian Korab©

(above) This compact attic family room is made more cozy by built-in cabinetry and a window seat.

(left) A fireplace and broad hearth create a strong focal point in this spacious family room.

(opposite) Creative design turned this basement space into a well-balanced family room. Oversize soffits conceal mechanicals and make an interesting ceiling, and custom wood trim dresses up structural columns.

Bob Perron©

Playroom

Basements and attics are treasured locations for playrooms. Building a playroom is easy, but making the space safe, practical, and fun for kids takes some thoughtful planning. Following are some ideas and tips that can help.

Design a playroom with separate play areas. This helps children organize their toys and keeps clutter to a minimum (elementary classrooms are set up in the same way). Some popular types of areas include spaces for reading; make-believe/dress-up; television, movies, and music; and crafts.

A reading area should include a variety of bookcases. For young children, built-ins are better than freestanding bookcases, which can be accidentally pulled down. Anchor any freestanding bookcases to the wall, and remove the lower shelves to prevent climbing.

A make-believe/dress-up area may have low built-in cabinetry, great for storing tubs full of plastic dishes, pots and pans, and other items children can use for make-believe. Low-mounted wall pegs are great for hanging costumes and dress-up clothes. You can furnish the area with a child-sized table and chair set.

Photo courtesy of Williams-Sonoma/Pottery Barn

Equipment in a television/movie/music area is best housed in a locking built-in entertainment center. This prevents little hands from inserting items into the VCR or playing with the television or stereo. Make sure there are no glass cabinet doors.

A crafts area should include cabinetry and a large utility table. Fill plastic tubs with art supplies and craft items. For fun, consider painting a wall with chalkboard paint. This special paint, available at paint stores, turns any smooth wall into a chalkboard.

The location of a playroom is an important consideration. If you have small children, you may want the room within sight of a home office or family room, allowing you the freedom to work while you supervise the children. If the playroom must be in a remote location, you can install a home monitor or intercom system for communication between rooms.

Photo courtesy of Williams-Sonoma/Pottery Barn

(above) Kid-size furniture and a playhouse become the center of activity in a playroom.

(left) A playroom is a great place for children to create and display their own artwork. Low shelves give children easy access to supplies.

(opposite) Casual furnishings and playful decorations make this playroom a comfortable place for children and adults.

Bedroom

Attic and basement spaces offer some unique advantages for bedrooms. Because basements tend to be somewhat dark and cool, they can be ideal environments for sleeping. Basements are also quiet, especially standard basements that are mostly below grade. To maintain this quiet, make sure the floor surface directly above the bedroom is carpeted and the floor joists between are filled with insulation.

An attic bedroom can be a cozy corner room tucked in under the eaves or a lofty space with a high, peaked ceiling. Attic bedrooms are great for children, because most kids like private places to call their own. If you need more space for an attic bedroom, consider adding a dormer. A dormer is a structure that projects from a roof, consisting of a small roof, two triangular side walls, and a front wall that contains one or more vertical windows. Dormers create sunny alcoves and add usable floor space.

When planning a bedroom, there are some important building code requirements to keep in mind. By definition, bedrooms are sleeping rooms, and as such they must have a means of *egress,* or

(above) Operable skylights in an attic bedroom provide ventilation and views of the stars. (opposite) A high ceiling and furnished cubby help this modest attic space feel more roomy.

emergency escape, leading directly to the outdoors (see below). Most codes also require that every bedroom have a smoke alarm inside the room and another outside each separate sleeping area; both must be hard-wired to a house circuit. The local code may have additional requirements for bedroom safety, so check with the building department in your area.

EGRESS WINDOWS

Attic and basement bedrooms—and all other sleeping areas—must have an approved exit for emergency escape in addition to the main entry. In most bedrooms, this is provided by egress windows. An egress window must provide a clear opening of 5.7 sq. ft., with a minimum width of 20" and a minimum height of 24". They can be no higher than 44" above the floor and must be easy to open from the inside without a key.

Basement egress windows that are underground must open into a window well that meets strict specifications (see page 75). To provide safe escape from an attic egress window, store a safety ladder near the window. These roll-up ladders hook onto window frames and roll out to the ground below.

Doors can also provide means of egress, as long as they are at least 36" wide and 6 ft., 8" tall.

Bathroom

No matter how you use the space in a finished basement or attic, if your family will be spending more time there, you're going to need a bathroom. Bathrooms require careful planning—among other considerations, there are numerous code issues involved. In addition, the location of the bathroom can have a significant effect on the cost of the project, although the time and money spent will be more than repaid in convenience and added value to your home.

The most important decision involved in planning a new bathroom is where to put it. If possible, place the bathroom near existing plumbing lines so it will be easier to connect the fixture drains. In an attic, the best location may be above an existing bathroom or kitchen; in a basement, the bathroom should be near the main waste-vent stack and house drain. Your basement may have been built with drain stub-outs in place, which generally determines the location for you.

There are many building code specifications for bathrooms, but for your initial planning, follow the general clearances for fixtures (see below). These can give you an idea of how much space you'll need. As for overall room dimensions, keep in mind that most building codes permit a lower ceiling in bathrooms—typically 7 ft. The floor space required for your bathroom will largely depend on the types and number of fixtures included, but as suggested minimums, a powder room should be at least 16 sq. ft., and a full bath requires about 40 sq. ft. of floor space. A standard tub takes up about 5 feet in one direction. To provide space for a wheelchair to move around, plan 5 × 5 ft. of clear space.

Photo courtesy of Velux-America Inc.

Bob Perron©

(top) This bright attic bathroom has a skylight that opens for ventilation.

(bottom) Even the space under a staircase may provide enough room for a small half-bath.

(opposite) An attic bathroom may work best tucked in underneath a dormer.

BATHROOM LAYOUT

The following are some general code guidelines for positioning bathroom fixtures (consult the local building department for specific regulations in your area):

Sinks must be at least 4" from side walls and have 21" of clearance in front. Sinks should be spaced 4" away from neighboring sinks and toilets, and 2" away from bathtubs. Toilets must be centered 15" from side walls and tubs, with 21" clearance in front. Shower stalls must be at least 30 × 30", with 24" of clearance in front of the shower opening.

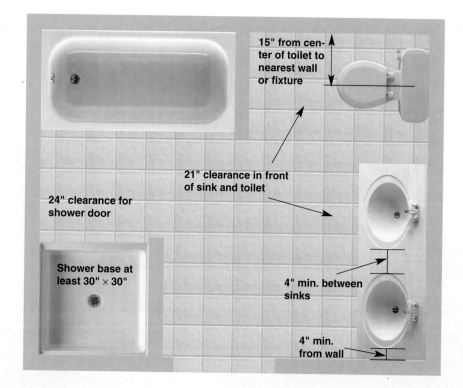

15" from center of toilet to nearest wall or fixture

21" clearance in front of sink and toilet

24" clearance for shower door

Shower base at least 30" × 30"

4" min. between sinks

4" min. from wall

In-law Suite

More and more families are expanding their living space to include in-law suites for aging relatives. An in-law suite can be as simple as a bedroom with an adjoining bathroom or as elaborate as an apartment, complete with a kitchen and separate living areas. It's important that a suite provide comfortable, safe, and private space for its occupants.

With ample room that's removed from the main flow of traffic through the house, an attic or basement can be ideal for an in-law suite; however, access is a primary consideration. A stairway to an attic or basement suite should meet or exceed code specifications, and it's a good idea to include a handrail on each side of the stairwell. Or, you can provide automatic travel up and down stairs by installing a stair lift. A walkout basement with an outside entrance offers additional access.

The types of rooms and facilities included in an in-law suite will determine how independently it functions. A full-accommodation suite should have a well-equipped kitchen, laundry facilities, and perhaps an entertainment room. Scaling back a little, you may include only a *morning kitchen* for food preparation. A morning kitchen typically consists of a sink, a small refrigerator, a microwave, and a coffee maker set into built-in cabinetry.

If you're planning a suite for elderly or physically disabled family members, safety and usability concerns should guide your design. Some safety features will be prescribed by the building code. For example, a sleeping area must have an egress window or door that allows emergency escape in case of fire (see page 16). Other elements will be dictated by the residents' needs. One common consideration is providing adequate lighting: Keep in mind that, on average, an eighty-year-old person needs ten times more light to see than an eighteen-year-old person. The tips shown below list some Universal Design specifications that can help you customize your in-law suite to ensure comfort and safety.

(top) An in-law suite doesn't have to be large: This bed tucked under a dormer is part of a studio-style suite.

(bottom) Separate living areas, such as this well-lighted reading room, make a suite more like a private residence.

(opposite) An outside entrance to a suite in a walkout basement can provide an added feeling of independence and privacy.

Tips For Universal Design

Universal Design is aimed at making houses and their facilities safe and comfortable for people of all sizes, ages, and abilities. For more information on Universal Design, contact the National Kitchen and Bath Association (see page 157).

- Construct doorways with at least 32"-wide clearance; allow 18-24" on the handle-side of doorways.

- Install low countertops to accommodate working while sitting or for the use of wheelchairs; provide adequate knee space.

- Add extra lighting both indoors and outdoors—near walkways, stairs, and entrances.

- Connect lights to automatic timers.

- Install rocker-type light switches (instead of toggle switches).

- Add a shower stall with grab bars, a shower seat, an anti-scald faucet, and a hand-held sprayer.

- Replace two-handled faucets with single-lever faucets.

- Mount grab bars near bathtubs and toilets.

- Install a telephone or intercom in the bathroom, for use in emergencies.

- Replace outside stairways with ramps, or landscape entrances with gradual slopes.

Home Theater

Home theaters originated as miniature movie theaters in upscale homes, complete with multi-level seating and enormous front-projection screens. Today's home theaters represent a broader range—some are as simple as a large TV and basic component system installed in a room that looks like an ordinary family room. And depending on the system you choose, adding a home theater can be a great do-it-yourself project.

The first planning issue is deciding where to put your home theater. An attic may serve well as a theater space, but generally a basement is a better choice. Basements typically have limited natural light—darkness is best for movie-watching. And perhaps most important, basement floors and walls are already soundproofed, so it's easier to contain the booming sounds produced by the system's multiple speakers.

Although your home theater can be used for other activities, make the viewing experience a priority. Your theater room should measure at least 12 × 15 ft., and will offer better acoustics if it's rectangular rather than square. The layout of

the system and furniture is critical to the viewing experience. The drawing on page 24 shows a suggested layout of home theater seating for a standard system. Keep in mind that different systems require different room sizes and configurations for best performance; it's a good idea to shop for a system before you finalize your room plans. (See page 25 for an overview of typical system components.)

Photo courtesy of Ultimate Electronics-Audio King-Sound Track

The surfaces of the room also have an effect on the sound quality. As a general rule, avoid hard surfaces that reflect sound. Carpeting is the best floor covering, but if you want a wood or tile floor, use throw rugs to absorb some of the sound waves. Add curtains over any windows to block light and absorb sound. Soft wall hangings and bookshelves also reduce sound interference. To minimize sound transmission to other rooms in the house, soundproof the ceiling and any framed walls in the theater room.

If you install your home theater system yourself, run the wiring and cables while the framing is still exposed. And because you may want to make adjustments to the speaker placement after the walls and ceiling are finished, run extra wire to each speaker location.

(above) Small system packages with free-standing speakers are easy to install and can be moved if necessary.

(left) Slide-out racks attractively conceal system components and provide easy access to wiring connections.

(opposite) The custom-built wall in this home theater holds the theater system, as well as recessed shelving and a wet bar.

Karen Melvin©

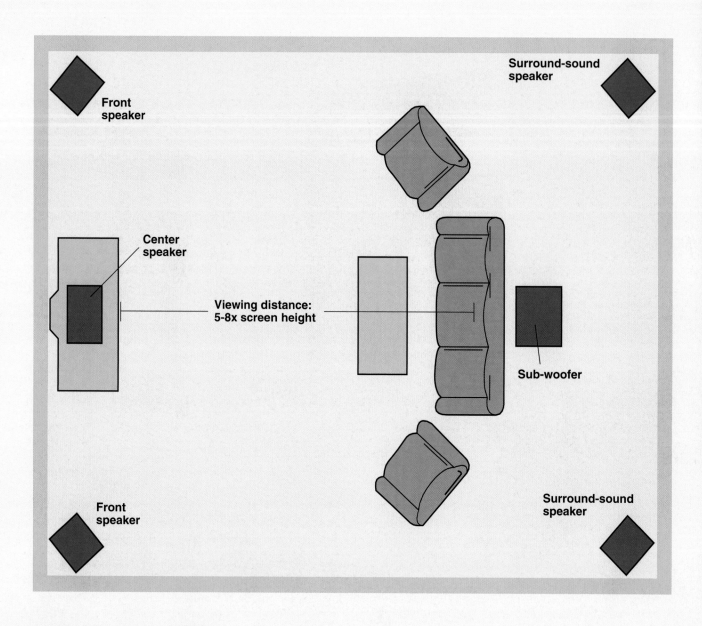

Front
speaker

Surround-sound
speaker

Center
speaker

Viewing distance:
5-8x screen height

Sub-woofer

Front
speaker

Surround-sound
speaker

HOME THEATER LAYOUT

Here are some general guidelines for arranging home theater equipment and furniture. To find the best layout for your system, experiment with different viewing positions and speaker arrangements.

Place the TV or viewing screen in the center of one of the short walls of the room (if the room is rectangular). Usually the best seating position is directly in front of the screen or just to the side of center. To determine the best viewing distance, measure the height of the screen: Place your seating at a distance five to eight times the screen height. For example, if your screen is 24" tall, the best viewing distance will be somewhere between 10 and 16 ft. from the screen. Also, the screen should be at eye-level for seated viewers.

A typical home theater system uses five speakers, each channeling one part of the video sound. Place the two front speakers a few feet equally left and right of the screen. These speakers reproduce music and

sound effects. Position the center speaker, which transmits most of the dialogue, just above or below the screen, so speech seems to come directly from the actors. The two surround-sound speakers provide audio atmosphere, such as the sound of an airplane flying overhead. Position these speakers behind your seating area at ear height or above and slightly to the sides, left and right. Since surround-sound speakers are generally smaller, you often can mount them onto or inside a wall. A subwoofer is an optional sixth speaker that is dedicated to low bass frequencies. To get its best effect, place a subwoofer in a corner near the front of the room or near your seats.

Position light fixtures in the room so they are not reflected in the screen and do not diminish the picture clarity. Wall sconces that are shaded upward and other types of indirect lighting work best. Use dimmer switches to get just the right level of lighting.

SYSTEM COMPONENTS

The basic home theater setup consists of an audio system (receiver and speakers), a video player (DVD or VCR), and a TV or viewing screen. For best performance, use high quality speaker cable for your speakers and coaxial cable for the video and TV.

Audio system. *The heart of the audio system (top) is a multi-channel, audio/video receiver. This has five channels for delivering amplified power to each of the speakers. A receiver should have 100 watts per channel and a Dolby Digital decoder (for processing the audio channels). Most sound systems include five speakers, or "satellites," and a subwoofer, which typically has a built-in amplifier. Since all three front speakers are close to the screen, they should be magnetically shielded to avoid distorting the picture.*

Video player. *The two main types of video player are DVD (Digital Video Disk) player (bottom) and VCR (Video Cassette Recorder). DVDs play movies from disks similar to audio CDs. With twice the resolution of a VCR, a DVD is the preferred playback source. However, most DVD players do not have a record function, so if you want to tape movies or shows from your television, you'll also need a VCR. With a dual-deck VCR, you can watch a movie on your screen while simultaneously recording a TV show.*

Screen.
Direct-view TVs are the most common for average home theater systems. These are similar to standard, glass-tube televisions, and they produce bright, clear pictures at a reasonable cost. A 27" screen (measured diagonally) is about the minimum size for a home theater; a 40" screen is preferred.

Rear-projection TVs boast a bigger screen (40 to 70"), but the picture may be less crisp than on direct-view models. Rear-projection units project the video image from behind the screen

Front-projection units transmit images across a room to an opaque screen, much like a traditional movie theater setup. Screen sizes can run 100" or larger, and the systems are very expensive.

Digital TVs are increasing in popularity, due to changes in broadcasting technology. These produce clear images, but they cost more than standard analog units. As an alternative, you can purchase a digital converter to view digital broadcasts on an analog TV.

Plasma TVs (above) are large screens with slim profiles (just 4" deep) that can sit on the floor or hang on a wall. These are high-quality units, but very expensive.

Recreation Room

The basement has always been a favorite location for a recreation room. Its solid floor and walls make it suitable for rowdy activity, and it's usually the only room in the house large enough to accommodate a pool table. Plus, because it's situated away from the main flow of traffic, the basement is an ideal place to unwind. An attic also offers seclusion and a break from routine, but not the sturdiness of masonry construction found in basements. Consequently, attics are better suited to rooms designed for less vigorous recreation—a sunny card room or a quiet corner spa might be just right for your attic.

Home gyms are popular additions for basements. The concrete floors in basements can support heavy equipment and reduce vibration noise from exercise machines, and they can easily withstand shock from dropped weights. Basement gyms will also stay relatively cool—and comfort is an important issue for exercise rooms. If a gym is not comfortable or is located in a secluded corner that you never see (out of sight—out of mind), you may be less inclined to use it. Be sure to provide plenty of lighting and ventilation for safety and comfort, and consider installing a TV or stereo system to keep you company during workouts.

If you're planning to add a pool room in your basement, make sure the table and cues fit the dimensions of the room (playing pool in cramped quarters is no fun). See the chart below for the recommended room dimensions for various pool table sizes. Note that the most popular size of pool table is 4 × 8 ft., and the standard cue length is 57".

(top) A whirlpool tub set next to a window makes a relaxing retreat.

(above) Built-in wood cabinetry and a fireplace can give your basement the atmosphere of a classic billiards room.

(opposite) Wall-mounted mirrors visually expand a home gym, and they help you monitor your form as you exercise.

Ideal Room Size: Per Table by Cue Length

Table size (Playing Surface)	Room Size		
	48" Cues	52" Cues	57" Cues
3'6" × 7' (39 × 78")	11'3" × 14'6"	11'11" × 15'2"	12'9" × 16'
4' × 8' (44 × 92")	11'8" × 15'4"	12'4" × 16'	13'2" × 16'10"
4' × 8' OS (46 × 92")	12' × 15'8"	12'6" × 16'4"	13'4" × 17'2"
4'6" × 9' (50 × 100")	12'2" × 16'4"	12'10" × 17'	13'8" × 17'10"

Getting Started

Although many attics and basements are good candidates for finishing, not all are suitable. Some spaces are simply too small or have very low ceilings or problems like flooding that make the investment too risky. If you've been thinking about remodeling, chances are the space is usable, but it could require some expensive preparation work to ensure safety and structural integrity over time. Of course, it's best to know this early in the process. Therefore, the first step is to evaluate the space to find out what you have to work with, what changes are necessary, and how much everything will cost.

The primary gauge by which to measure your attic or basement is the local building code. This code describes all the requirements for livable spaces in your area, and it governs every aspect of your project. There are code specifications for everything from minimum headroom to how many electrical receptacles you'll need in your new family room. For personal reference, you can probably find a copy of the building code at a local library, but for the most part, you'll learn about the requirements from the officials at the building department. They can also warn you about problems specific to your area, such as a high water table or expansive soil.

This section shows you the basic elements to look for as you evaluate your basement or attic. Much of this you can check out yourself; other matters may require professional examination. If your attic or basement passes your evaluation, hire an architect, engineer, or building contractor to have a look at the space and the elements that will be affected by the project. You can also use your home's original blueprints to learn about the basic structure of the house and locate mechanical rough-ins without cutting holes in the walls. If you don't have blueprints, contact your home's builder or the city office to get a copy of them.

When you've finished the evaluation stage and are ready to start remodeling, take some time to plan the project and draft a construction schedule. This step includes designing the space, getting the building permits, and establishing an order for all of the construction that follows. It's a challenging part of the remodeling process, but creating an effective plan is essential to a successful project.

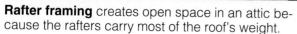

Rafter framing creates open space in an attic because the rafters carry most of the roof's weight.

Trusses are made of interconnected cords and webs, which close off most of the attic space.

Evaluating Your Attic

Start your attic evaluation with a quick framing inspection. If the roof is framed with rafters, you can continue to the next test. If it's built with trusses, however, consider remodeling your basement instead. The problem is that the internal supports in trusses leave too little space to work with, and trusses cannot be altered.

The next step is to check for headroom and overall floor space. Most building codes call for 7½ ft. of headroom over 50% of the "usable" floor space, which is defined as any space with a ceiling height of at least 5 ft. Remember that these minimums apply to the finished space—after the flooring and ceiling surfaces are installed. Other things can affect headroom, as well, such as reinforcing the floor frame, and increasing rafter depth for strength or insulation.

You may also find various supports in your attic

that are there to strengthen your roof but may limit your space. *Collar ties* are horizontal boards that join two rafters together in the upper third of the rafter span. They prevent rafter uplift in high winds. Often collar ties can be moved up a few inches but cannot be removed. *Rafter ties* join rafters in the lower third of their span to prevent spreading. In most attics, the ceiling or floor joists serve as rafter ties. *Purlins* are horizontal boards that run at right angles to the rafters and are supported by struts. These systems shorten the rafter span, allowing the use of smaller lumber for the rafters. You may be allowed to substitute kneewalls for purlins and struts. If you'll need to have any support system altered or moved, consult an architect or engineer.

The rafters themselves also need careful examination. Inspect them for signs of stress or damage, such as cracks, sagging, and insect infestation. Look for dark areas indicating roof leaks. If you find leaks or you know your roofing is past its useful life, have it repaired or replaced before you start the fin-

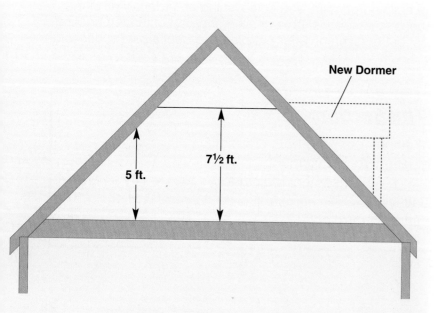

Habitable rooms must be at least 70 sq. ft. total and measure at least 7 ft. in any one direction. To meet headroom requirements, 50% of the usable floor space must have a ceiling height of 7½ ft.

You can add to your floor space and headroom by adding protruding windows called *dormers*. In addition to space, dormers add light and ventilation to your attic.

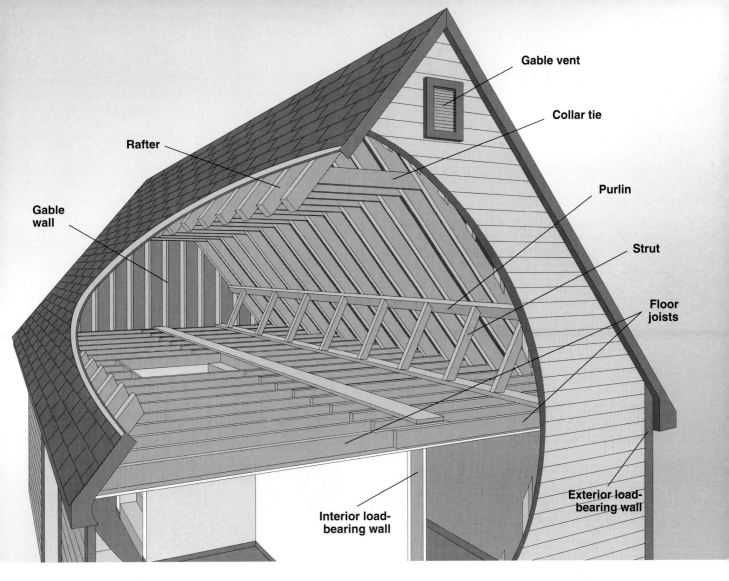

Gable vent

Collar tie

Rafter

Purlin

Gable wall

Strut

Floor joists

Interior load-bearing wall

Exterior load-bearing wall

ishing process. And even if the rafters appear healthy, they may be too small to support the added weight of finish materials. Small rafters can also be a problem if they don't provide enough room for adequate insulation.

At this point, it's a good idea to have a professional check the structural parts of your attic, including the rafters and everything from the floor down. In some cases, finishing an attic is like adding a story to your home, which means that the structure must have adequate support for the new space. Attic floors are often built as ceiling frames for the level below and are not intended to support living space. Floors can be strengthened with additional joists, known as *sister* joists or with new joists installed between the existing ones.

Support for the attic floor is provided by the load-bearing walls below and, ultimately, by the foundation. If these elements can't support the finished attic, they'll need to be reinforced. This may be as simple as strengthening the walls with plywood panels or as complicated as adding support posts and beams or reinforcing the foundation.

In addition to these structural matters, there are a few general code requirements you should keep in mind as you inspect your attic. If you plan to add a bedroom, it will need at least one exit to the outside. This can be a door leading to an outside stairwell or an egress window (see page 16). Most codes also have minimum requirements for ventilation and natural light, which means you may have to add windows or skylights.

One of the largest expenses of finishing an attic is in providing access: You'll need a permanent stairway at least 36" wide, with room for a 36" landing at the top and bottom. This is an important planning issue because adding a stairway affects the layout and traffic patterns of the attic as well as the floor below. (See page 37 for more information on stairways.)

Finally, take an inventory of existing mechanicals in your attic. While plumbing and wiring runs can be moved relatively easily, other features, such as chimneys, must be incorporated into your plans. This is a good time to have your chimney inspected by a fire official and to obtain the building code specifications for framing around chimneys.

Evaluating Your Basement

The two things that put an end to the most basement finishing plans are inadequate headroom and moisture. Begin your evaluation by measuring from the basement floor to the bottom of the floor joists above. Most building codes require habitable rooms to have a finished ceiling height of 7½ ft., measured from the finished floor to the lowest part of the finished ceiling. However, obstructions, such as beams, soffits, and pipes, (spaced at least 4 ft. on center) usually can hang down 6" below that height. Hallways and bathrooms typically need at least 7-ft. ceilings.

While it's impractical to add headroom in a basement, there are some ways of working around the requirements. Ducts and pipes often can be moved, and beams and other obstructions can be incorporated into walls or hidden in closets or other uninhabitable spaces. Also, some codes permit lower ceiling heights in rooms with specific purposes, such as recreation rooms. If headroom is a problem, talk to the local building department before you dash your dreams.

If your basement passes the headroom test, you can move on to the next issue: moisture. For a full discussion on this critical matter, see *Dealing with Basement Moisture*, on pages 34-36. Be aware that moisture problems must be corrected before you start the finishing process.

A well-built basement is structurally sound and provides plenty of support for finished space, but before you cover up the walls, floor, and ceiling, check for potential problems. Inspect the masonry carefully. Large cracks may indicate shifting of the soil around the foundation; severely bowed or out-of-plumb walls may be structurally unsound. Small cracks usually cause moisture problems rather than structural woes, but they should be sealed to prevent further cracking. Contact an engineer or foundation contractor for help with foundation problems. If you have an older home, you may find sagging floor joists overhead or rotted wood posts or beams; any defective wood framing will have to be reinforced or replaced.

Your basement's mechanicals are another important consideration. The locations of water heaters, pipes, wiring, circuit boxes, furnaces, and ductwork can have a significant impact on the cost and difficulty of your project. Can you plan around components, or will they have to be moved? Is there enough headroom to install a suspended ceiling so mechanicals can remain accessible? Or, will you have to reroute pipes and ducts to increase headroom? Electricians and HVAC contractors can assess your systems and suggest modifications.

Aside from being dark and scary places, unfinished basements often harbor toxic elements. One of the most common is *radon*, a naturally occurring radioactive gas that is odorless and colorless. It's believed that prolonged exposure to high levels of radon can cause lung cancer. The Environmental Protection Agency (see page 157) has free publications to help you test for radon and take steps to reduce the levels in your house. For starters, you can perform a "short-term" test using a kit from a hardware store or home center. Look for the phrase "Meets EPA requirements" to ensure the test kit is accurate. Keep in mind that short-term tests are not as conclusive as profes-

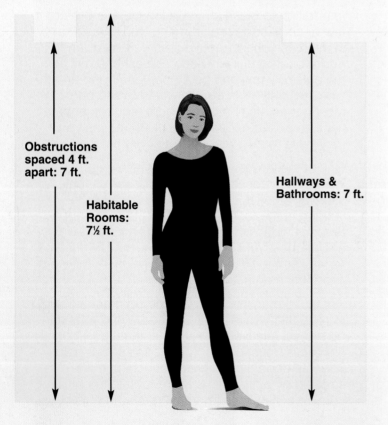

Obstructions spaced 4 ft. apart: 7 ft.

Habitable Rooms: 7½ ft.

Hallways & Bathrooms: 7 ft.

Basement headroom is often limited by beams, ducts, pipes, and other elements. Typical minimums for ceiling height are shown here: 7½ ft. for habitable rooms; 7 ft. for bathrooms and hallways; 7 ft. for obstructions spaced no less than 4 ft. apart.

Tips for Evaluating Your Basement

Rerouting service lines and mechanicals adds quickly to the expense of a project, so consider your options carefully.

Weakened or undersized joists and other framing members must be reinforced or replaced.

Old insulation containing asbestos poses a serious health risk if it is deteriorating or is disturbed.

Minor cracks such as these in masonry walls and floors usually can be sealed and forgotten, while severe cracking may indicate serious structural problems.

sional, long-term tests. If your test reveals high levels of radon, contact a radon specialist.

Another basement hazard is insulation containing asbestos, which was commonly used in older homes for insulating ductwork and heating pipes. In most cases, this insulation can be left alone provided it's in good condition and is protected from damage. If you fear the insulation in your basement poses a hazard, contact an asbestos abatement contractor to have it evaluated or safely removed.

Also check the local codes for exits from finished basements—most codes require two. The stairway commonly serves as one exit, while the other can be a door to the outside, an egress window (see page 16), or a code-compliant *bulkhead* (an exterior stairway with cellar doors). Each bedroom will also need an egress window or door for escape.

Stairways must also meet local code specifications. If yours doesn't, you'll probably have to hire someone to rebuild it. See page 37 for an overview of typical staircase requirements.

As a final note, if you're planning to finish the basement in a new house, ask the builder how long you should wait before starting the project. Poured concrete walls and floors need time to dry out before they can be covered. Depending on where you live, you may be advised to wait up to two years, just to be safe.

Dealing with Basement Moisture

Basement moisture can destroy your efforts to create functional living space. Over time, even small amounts of moisture can rot framing, turn wallboard to mush, and promote the growth of mold and mildew. Fortunately, most moisture problems can be resolved, but any measures you take must prove effective before you proceed with your project. Ensuring your basement will stay dry throughout the seasons may require waiting a year or more, but considering the time and money involved, it will be worth the delay.

Basement moisture appears in two forms: condensation and seepage. Condensation comes from airborne water vapor that turns to water when it contacts cold surfaces. Common sources of vapor include humid outdoor air, poorly ventilated appliances, damp walls, and traces of water released from concrete. Seepage is water that enters the basement by infiltrating cracks in the foundation or by leeching through the masonry. Typically caused by ineffective exterior drainage, seepage comes from rain or groundwater that collects around the foundation or from a rising water table.

If you've had a wet basement in the past, you may know when to expect moisture but may not know where it's coming from. Even if your basement has been dry for a long time, look for evidence of moisture problems. Typical signs include peeling paint, white residue on masonry, mildew stains, sweaty windows and pipes, rusted appliance feet, rotted wood near the floor, buckled floor tile, and strong mildew odors.

Once you determine you have a moisture problem, locate the source. The first step is to test for condensation and seepage: Lay a square of plastic or aluminum foil on the floor and another on an exterior foundation wall, and tape down all four sides of each. Check the squares after two days. If moisture has formed on top of a square, you probably have a condensation problem; moisture on the underside indicates seepage.

To reduce condensation, run a dehumidifier in the dampest area of the basement. Insulate cold-water pipes to prevent condensate drippage, and make sure your dryer and other appliances have vents running to the outside. Central A/C service in the basement can help reduce vapor during warm, humid months.

Cracks in walls

Poorly designed window well

Improper grading

Cracks in slab

Leaky joints

Footing

Common causes of basement moisture include improper grading around the foundation, inadequate or faulty gutter systems, humidity and condensation, cracks in foundation walls, leaky joints between structural elements, and poorly designed window wells. More extensive problems include large cracks in the foundation, damaged or missing drain tiles, a high water table, or the presence of underground streams. Often, a combination of factors is at fault.

Crawlspaces also can promote condensation, as warm, moist air enters through crawlspace vents and meets the cooler interior air. Crawlspace ventilation is a source of ongoing debate, and there's no universal method that applies to all climates. It's best to ask the local building department or an experienced local contractor for advice on this matter.

Solutions for preventing seepage range from simple do-it-yourself projects to expensive professional jobs requiring excavation and foundation work. Since it's often difficult to determine the source of seeping water, it makes sense to try some common cures before calling in professional help.

Begin by checking your yard's grade. The first 6 ft. of ground around the foundation should slope away at a rate of 1" per foot and at least ¾" per foot beyond that. Use a level, a long board, and a tape measure to check the grade. If the slope is inadequate, build up the ground around the foundation to improve drainage.

Next, inspect your downspouts and gutters. Give the gutters a thorough cleaning, and patch any holes. Make sure the gutters slope toward the downspouts at about 1⁄16" per foot. And most important, add downspout extensions and splashblocks to keep roof runoff at least 8 ft. away from the foundation.

Window wells allow water into a basement, and covering them with removable plastic covers is the easiest way to keep them dry. If you prefer to leave wells uncovered, add a gravel layer and a drain to the bottom of the well. Clean the well regularly to remove moisture-heavy debris. See page 75 for more information on window wells.

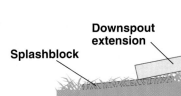

(above) **Test for condensation and seepage** by taping a square of aluminum foil to the floor and a wall. Moisture on top of the foil indicates condensation; moisture underneath reveals seepage.

(right) **Improve your gutter system and foundation grade** to prevent rainwater and snow-melt from flooding your basement. Keep gutters clean and straight. Make sure there's a downspout for every 50 ft. of roof eave, and extend downspout piping 8 ft. from the foundation. Build up the grade around the foundation so that it carries water away from the house.

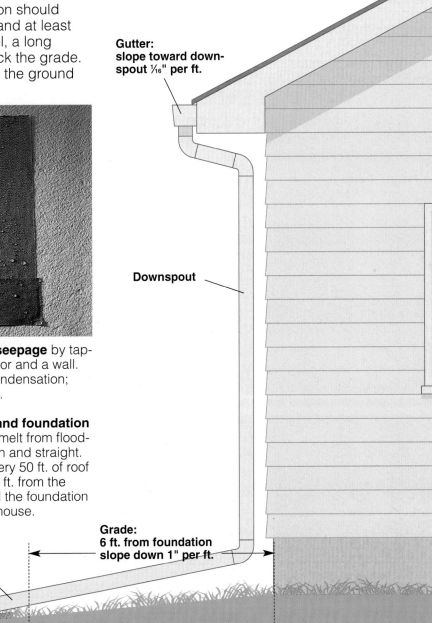

Gutter:
slope toward down-
spout 1⁄16" per ft.

Downspout

Grade:
6 ft. from foundation
slope down 1" per ft.

Downspout
extension

Splashblock

To help stop seepage from inside the basement, patch cracks in the foundation walls and floors. Use waterproof masonry sealant for cracks under ¼" wide, and use hydraulic cement for larger cracks. Whole-wall interior coatings, such as masonry waterproofer, may also help reduce basement moisture. However, be aware that while sealing the foundation from the inside can help block occasional and light moisture, it will not solve serious moisture problems, regardless of the manufacturer's claims.

If these simple measures don't correct your moisture problems, you must consider more extensive action. Serious water problems are typically handled by footing drains or sump systems. Footing drains are installed around the foundation's perimeter, near the footing, and they drain out to a distant area of the yard. These usually work in conjunction with waterproof coatings on the foundation walls. Sump systems use an interior under-slab drain pipe to collect water in a pit. From there, the water is sent outside by an electric sump pump.

Find out if your house has one of these systems in place. It may be that your footing drain pipes

Fill cracks in the foundation with masonry waterproofer or hydraulic cement. This helps reduce minor seepage and prevents further cracking.

are clogged with silt or have been damaged by tree roots. If you have a sump pit in your basement floor, but no pump or discharge pipe in place, you may need to install a pump and drain lines. (Be aware that there may be regulations about where the sump pump drains.)

Installing a new drainage system is expensive and must be done properly. Adding a sump system involves breaking up the concrete floor along the basement's perimeter, digging a trench, and laying a perforated drain pipe in a bed of gravel. After the sump pit is installed, the floor is patched with new concrete. Installing a footing drain is far more complicated. This involves digging out the foundation, installing gravel and drain pipe, and waterproofing the foundation walls. Thus, a footing drain is typically considered a last-resort measure.

Before you hire someone to install a drainage system, do some homework. Learn about the procedure the contractor has planned, and find out if it has been successful with other homes in your area. Check the contractor's references, and don't be afraid to get a second or third opinion before deciding.

Foundation drainage systems are designed to remove water that pools around footings. Footing drains collect water from outside the footing and carry it out to daylight. Sump systems collect water underneath the basement floor and divert it into a pit. As the pit fills, a sump pump sends the water outside. Landscape drains remove water near the surface.

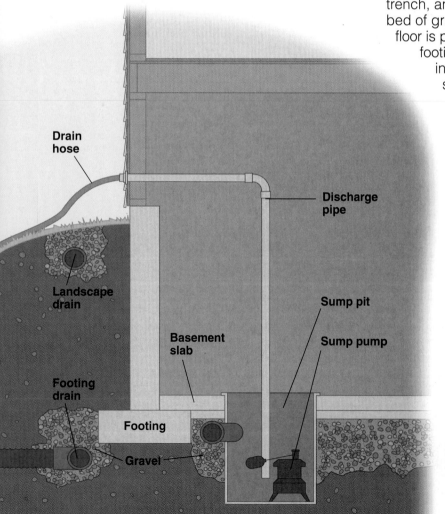

Drain hose

Discharge pipe

Landscape drain

Sump pit

Sump pump

Basement slab

Footing drain

Footing

Gravel

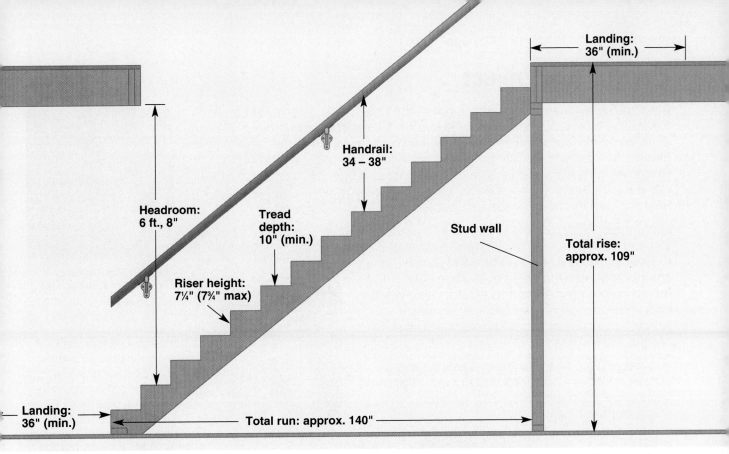

Stairway code requirements typically call for a 36"-wide stairway with 6 ft., 8" of headroom and uniform treads and risers. The ends of staircases are anchored to a cleat at the bottom and doubled floor joists at the top.

Stairways

An attic or basement finishing project requires safe access—both during the construction phase and after completion. And while you may have an existing stairway that's seen plenty of use, chances are it doesn't meet building code requirements for finished spaces. If there is no stairway, you'll need to plan carefully to find the best location for a new one. And because stairways must tie into the house framing, it's best to have this work done before anything else.

According to most building codes, basement and attic stairways must be at least 36" wide, with a minimum of 6 ft., 8" of headroom. Each step may have a maximum riser height of 7¾" and a minimum tread depth of 10". In addition, stairwells are required to have a 34"- to 38"-high handrail on at least one side, and a minimum 36"-deep landing at both the top and bottom of the stairs. And all stairways must be illuminated.

When evaluating your stairway, take into account your finishing plans. Steps must be as uniform as possible, with no more than a ⅜" variance in riser height. Thick tile or a basement subfloor that runs up to the first step will shorten the height of the first riser, creating an unsafe situa-

tion that doesn't meet code. You can adjust a new staircase to compensate for this, but an existing one doesn't offer such flexibility.

To plan a new staircase, consider how it will affect the surrounding spaces, as well as the traffic patterns, on both floors. The type of staircase you choose and where you put it will largely be determined by the available floor space. A standard straight-run stairway will occupy almost 50 sq. ft. of floor space on the lower level and 35 to 40 sq. ft. on the upper level. L- and U-shape stairways make 90° and 180° turns, respectively, allowing them to fit into smaller areas. *Winders* are L-shape stairs that make the turn with wedge-shape steps rather that a square platform. These allow a steeper rise in a confined area.

A spiral staircase offers a space-saving alternative for attic access. Spirals are available in stock sizes, or you can have them custom-built. However, spirals are not for everyone. They can be difficult to use for older people and young children, and some building codes limit their use as primary staircases.

Planning the Project

After you've evaluated your basement or attic and have determined that the space is usable, the next step is to plan the construction project. Having a complete construction plan enables you to view the entire project at a glance. It helps you identify potential problems, provides a sense of the time involved, and establishes a logical order of steps. Without a construction plan, it's easier to make costly errors, like closing up a wall with wallboard before the rough-ins are inspected.

It may help your planning to start with the end-results and work backwards. Think about each room in its finished state and consider how you will use it. What will you need for lighting? How will the space be heated? Is an emergency exit required? Defining the finished product now will also help you sort out the details, such as whether the cabinets should be installed before or after the flooring.

The general steps shown here follow a typical construction sequence. Your plan may differ at several points, but thinking through each of these steps will help you create a complete schedule.

1 Contact the building department. To avoid any unpleasant—and expensive—surprises, discuss your project with a building official. Find out what codes apply in your area and what you'll need to obtain the applicable permits. Explain how much of the work you plan to do yourself. (In some states, plumbing, electrical, and HVAC work must be done by licensed professionals.) Also determine what types of drawings you'll need to get permits.

2 Design the space. This is when you put your dreams to the test. Take measurements, make sketches, and test different layouts—find out what works and what doesn't. Consider all the necessary elements, such as headroom, lighting, mechanicals, and make sure everything adheres to local building codes. Determine whether mechanicals must be relocated.

3 Draw floor plans. Most attic and basement remodels can follow a simple set of plans that you can draw yourself. Start with copies of the original house plans, or simply measure the space and transfer the dimensions to graph paper. Basic floor plans should include dimensions of rooms, doors, and windows; all plumbing fixtures and HVAC equipment; electrical fixtures, receptacles, and switches; and closets, counters, and other built-in features. If you want professional help for this step, contact an architect, interior designer, remodeling contractor, or a design specialist at a home center.

4 Hire contractors. If you're getting help with your project, it's best to find and hire the contractors early in the process, as their schedules will affect yours. You may also need to have certain contractors pull their own permits at the building department. To avoid problems, make sure all of the contractors know exactly what work they are being hired to do and what work you will be doing yourself. Always check contractors' references and make sure they're licensed and insured before hiring them.

12 Make the final connections. Install the plumbing fixtures, and complete the drain and supply hook-ups. Make electrical connections, and install all fixtures, devices, and appliances. You're finished with the construction when you get the final inspection and approval from the building inspector.

5 Get the permits. Take your drawings, notes, and any required documents down to the building department, and obtain the permits for your project. Find out what work needs to be inspected and when to call for inspections. This is a critical step, as the permit process is required by law. Failure to get permits and the required inspections can make it difficult to sell your house and can negate your claim in insurance matters.

6 Make major structural & mechanical changes. Prepare the space for finishing by completing structural work and building new stairs, if necessary. Move mechanical elements and re-route major service lines. Also complete any rough-ins that must happen before the framing goes up, such as adding ducts, installing under-floor drains, and replacing old plumbing.

7 Frame the rooms. Build the floors, walls, and ceilings that establish your new rooms. In most cases, the floor will come first; however, you may want to rough-in service lines and insulate for soundproofing before installing the subfloor. Next come the walls. Cover foundation walls, and build partition walls and kneewalls. Build the rough openings for windows and doors. Enlarge existing basement window openings or cut new ones for egress windows. Install the windows.

8 Complete the rough-ins. Run DWV (drain, waste, and vent) and water and gas supply pipes. Install electrical boxes, and run the wiring. Install additional wiring, such as speaker wire and cables for phones, televisions, intercoms, and Internet access. Complete the HVAC rough-ins. Build soffits to enclose new service lines. For future reference, it's a good idea to take photographs or jot down some measurements of pipe and wire locations.

11 Add the finishing touches. Complete the general finish carpentry, such as installing doors, moldings and other woodwork, cabinets, and built-in shelving, and lay the floor coverings. The best order for these tasks will depend on the materials you're using and the desired decorative effects.

10 Finish the walls & ceilings. Make sure everything is in place before you cover up the framing. If you're installing wallboard, do the ceilings first, then the walls. Tape and finish the wallboard. Install other finish treatments. Texture, prime, and paint the wallboard when it's most convenient. If installing suspended ceilings, do so after finishing the walls.

9 Insulate. Insulate the walls, ceilings, and pipes for weatherizing and soundproofing. Install fiberglass insulation used as fireblocking. Make sure protector plates for pipes and wires running through framing are in place. Add vapor barriers as required by local code.

Basic Framing

Framing includes all the wood structures and surfaces that make up the rooms, hide the mechanicals, and enclose the unlivable spaces in your basement or attic. And, like all major construction elements, framing requires careful planning.

The first step is creating the layout of the finished space and making some drawings to work from. Some wall locations will be determined by existing elements, such as plumbing pipes, while others can follow a more aesthetic logic. Once your space is mapped out, you can begin work on the floor. Attic floors often need reinforcing to support the new living space. Basement floors usually need only a little patching or smoothing out, but you may decide to build a shallow wood subfloor over the concrete.

The types of walls you build will depend on the existing elements. You can cover basement foundation walls with furring strips attached to the masonry or with free-standing stud walls. In attics, short kneewalls define the sides of the space, and partition walls with angled top plates divide the areas in between. If you want a flat ceiling in your attic, frame it in before you build the partition walls. Door frames are easy to build into new interior walls, while window frames require modifying the existing framing or masonry. If your plans include a new skylight, see pages 126-131.

Before you start framing, check with the building department to find out where you'll need fireblocking. Fireblocking is typically solid framing lumber or unfaced fiberglass insulation that's nailed or stuffed into framing cavities. It slows the spread of fire from one floor to another. Most building codes require fireblocking in framed walls, vertical chases, and soffits. Also, make sure you haven't forgotten any preliminary rough-ins—like adding a new furnace duct—that will be much more difficult with new walls in place.

Planning the Framing

Use walls to define your new spaces. Walls can create quiet private retreats or comfortable bathrooms or serve as barriers between formal living areas and dusty, unfinished storage spaces. To determine where your walls should go, start with a thorough investigation of the unfinished space. All obstacles, such as mechanical systems, service lines, floor drains, support columns, chimneys, and roof framing, must be considered. As you work with different layouts, think about which of these elements can be enclosed by walls, which can be hidden within a wall or concealed by a soffit or chase, and which, if any, can be moved.

One technique to help you get started is to draw full-scale "walls" onto your basement floor, using children's sidewalk chalk (on wood attic floors, use wide masking tape instead of chalk). This can help you visualize the planned spaces and give you a better sense of room sizes. Complete the proposed layout in chalk, then walk through the rooms to test the traffic patterns. As you plan your rooms, keep in mind that most building codes require habitable rooms to have at least 70 sq. ft. of floor space and measure a minimum of 7 ft. in any direction.

The next step is to draw floor plans. This doesn't require drafting skills—just a tape measure, a ruler, graph paper, and some pencils. Simply measure your basement or attic floor space, then scale down the dimensions and transfer them to the graph paper. Add all obstacles, windows, doors, and other permanent fixtures. When everything is in place, start experimenting with different layouts. If you have your home's original blueprints, trace the floor plans onto tracing paper and work on new layouts from there.

Creating a successful layout takes time and often requires some creative problem-solving. To help generate ideas for your remodel, study the before-and-after drawings on page 43. While these floor plans may not look like your basement, they include many of the common elements and obstacles involved in a finishing project. They also show how carefully placed walls can transform an unfinished space into several livable areas that still leave room for storage and mechanical elements.

Use graph paper to sketch your wall layouts. Scale your floor plan (aerial view) drawings at ¼" equals 1 ft. For elevation drawings (wall details as viewed from the side), use a scale of ½" equals 1 ft.

Draw layouts onto your basement floor with sidewalk chalk. Use different colors to represent elements other than walls, such as doors, windows, and ceiling soffits. Remove the chalk with a damp rag.

Basement Layouts: Before and After

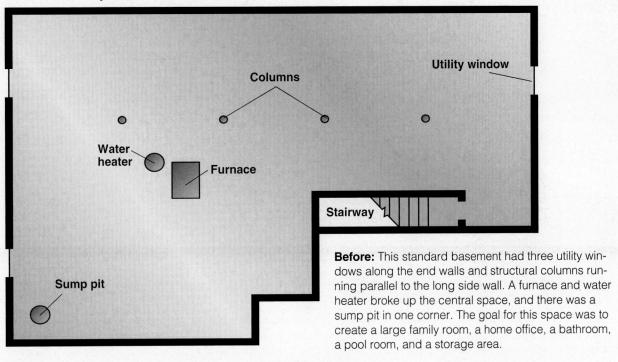

Before: This standard basement had three utility windows along the end walls and structural columns running parallel to the long side wall. A furnace and water heater broke up the central space, and there was a sump pit in one corner. The goal for this space was to create a large family room, a home office, a bathroom, a pool room, and a storage area.

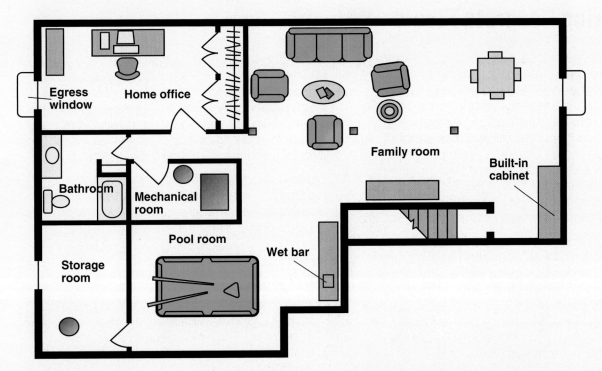

After: A few walls at one end of the basement define several of the new rooms. To add light to the home office, the existing window opening was expanded, and an egress window was installed, which allows the room to be used as a bedroom, as well. A larger window and well were also installed at the other end of the basement to provide light and a better view from the family room. One of the columns was hidden within the office wall, and the remaining three were wrapped with wood trim. The mechanical room contains the furnace and water heater, with plenty of space for servicing the units. Next to the office is a full bathroom, designed with a square layout that leaves a comfortable amount of space between the fixtures. The pool room occupies a well-defined space, where games won't disrupt activity in the family room. A wet bar can easily be accessed from both the pool room and family room. The stairway needed only a new handrail to become code-compliant. At the bottom of the stairs, a built-in cabinet provides storage and adds a decorative touch to the basement entrance.

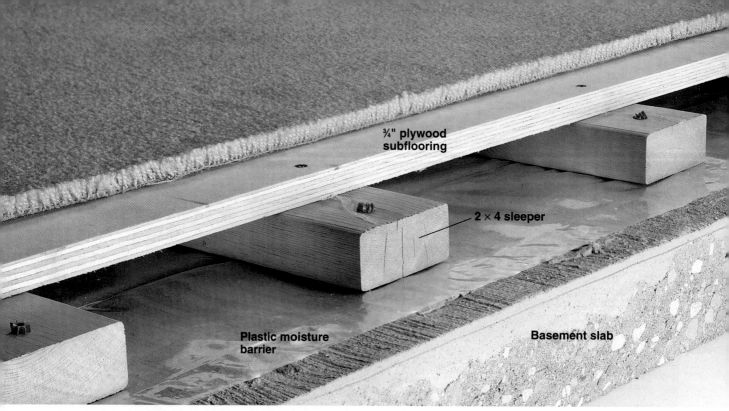

¾" plywood subflooring

2 × 4 sleeper

Plastic moisture barrier

Basement slab

Most basement floors need some preparation before flooring can be laid. Patching compound and floor leveler can smooth rough concrete, while a wood subfloor creates a new surface that feels like a framed wood floor.

Preparing Concrete Floors

How you prepare a concrete basement floor largely depends upon the condition of the floor, the type of floor covering you plan to use, and how you want the floor to feel underfoot. Flooring manufacturers have instructions for installing their products over concrete; follow these carefully, as they may affect the products' warranties. For this reason, it's best to decide on a floor covering before preparing the floor. Also, it's imperative that you solve any moisture problems with a concrete floor before covering it (see pages 34-36).

To lay flooring directly over concrete, prepare the floor so that it's smooth and flat. Fill cracks, holes, and expansion joints with a vinyl or cement-based floor patching compound. If the concrete is especially rough or uneven, apply a *floor leveler*—a self-leveling, cement-based liquid that fills deviations in the floor and dries to form a hard, smooth surface.

For a basement floor that doesn't feel like concrete, you can build a wood subfloor. A basement subfloor starts with a plastic moisture barrier and uses pressure-treated 2 × 4s laid flat—called *sleepers*—to act as floor joists. The sleepers are anchored to the concrete and topped with a layer of ¾" tongue-and-groove plywood.

A basement subfloor provides a flat, level surface that's more comfortable underfoot than con-

crete, and it serves as a nailing surface for certain types of flooring. A subfloor does take up valuable headroom, however, so you may want to save space by using 1 × 4 sleepers instead of 2 × 4s. Also consider how the added floor height will affect room transitions, as well as the bottom step of the basement stairs (see page 37).

Before laying out the sleepers, determine where the partition walls will go. If a wall will fall between parallel sleepers, add an extra sleeper for support under the planned wall location.

Everything You Need:

Tools: Vacuum, masonry chisel, trowel, floor scraper, long-nap paint roller, wheelbarrow, gage rake, 4-ft. level, circular saw, caulk gun, powder-actuated nailer, chalk line, drill, sledgehammer.

Materials: Vinyl floor patching compound, concrete primer, floor leveler, pressure-treated 2 × 4s, 6-mil polyethylene sheeting, packing tape, cedar shims, construction adhesive, concrete fasteners, ¾" T&G plywood, 2" wallboard screws.

How to Patch Concrete Floors

1 Clean the floor with a vacuum, and remove any loose or flaking concrete with a masonry chisel and hammer. Mix a batch of vinyl floor patching compound following manufacturer's directions. Apply the compound using a smooth trowel, slightly overfilling the cavity. Smooth the patch flush with the surface.

2 After the compound has cured fully, use a floor scraper to scrape the patched areas smooth.

How to Apply Floor Leveler

1 Remove any loose material and clean the concrete thoroughly; the surface must be free of dust, dirt, oils, and paint. Apply an even layer of concrete primer to the entire surface, using a long-nap paint roller. Let the primer dry completely.

2 Following the manufacturer's instructions, mix the floor leveler with water. The batch should be large enough to cover the entire floor area to the desired thickness (up to 1"). Pour the leveler over the floor.

3 Distribute the leveler evenly using a gage rake or spreader. Work quickly: The leveler begins to harden in 15 minutes. You can use a trowel to feather the edges and create a smooth transition with an uncovered area. Let the leveler dry for 24 hours.

How to Install a Basement Subfloor

1 Chip away loose or protruding concrete with a masonry chisel and hammer, then clean the floor thoroughly with a vacuum. Roll out strips of 6-mil polyethylene sheeting, extending them 3" up each wall. Overlap the strips by 6", then seal the seams with packing tape. Temporarily tape the edges along the walls. Be careful not to damage the sheeting.

2 Lay out pressure-treated 2 × 4s along the perimeter of the room. Position the boards ½" in from all walls (inset).

3 Cut the sleepers to fit between the perimeter boards, leaving a ¼" gap at each end. Position the first sleeper so it's center is 16" from the outside edge of the perimeter board. This ensures that one edge of the subflooring sheets will cover the perimeter board and the other edge will fall on the middle of a sleeper. Lay out the remaining sleepers using 16"-on-center spacing.

4 Where necessary, use tapered cedar shims to compensate for dips and variations in the floor. Set a 4-ft. level across the neighboring sleepers. Apply a small amount of construction adhesive to two shims of equal size. Slide the shims underneath the board from opposite sides until the board is level with the neighboring sleepers.

5 Fasten the perimeter boards and sleepers to the floor, using a powder-actuated nailer or masonry screws (see pages 53-54). Drive a single fastener through the center of each board every 16". The fastener heads should not protrude above the surface of the board. Fasten at all shim locations, making sure the fastener captures both shims.

6 Create a control line for the first row of plywood sheets by measuring out 49" from the wall and marking the outside sleeper at each end of the room. Snap a chalk line across the sleepers at the marks, perpendicular to the sleepers. Run a ¼"-wide bead of adhesive along the first six sleepers, stopping just short of the control line.

7 Position the first sheet of plywood, making sure the end is ½" away from the wall and the grooved edge is aligned with the control line. Fasten the sheet with 2" wallboard screws. Drive a screw every 6" along the edges and every 8" in the field of the sheet. Don't drive screws along the grooved edge until the next row of sheets is in place.

8 Install the remaining sheets in the first row, maintaining a ⅛" gap between the ends. Begin the second row with a half-sheet (4 ft.-long) so that the end joints between rows are staggered. Fit the tongue of the half sheet into the groove of the sheet behind it. If necessary, use a sledgehammer and a wood block to help close the joint (inset). After completing the second row, begin the third row with a full sheet, and so on, until the subfloor is complete.

Labels within image: Rafter, Floor joists, Exterior load-bearing wall, Interior load-bearing wall

Attic joists typically rest on top of exterior walls and on an interior load-bearing wall, where they overlap from side to side and are nailed together. Always use a sheet of plywood as a platform while working over open joists.

Building Attic Floors

Before you build the walls that will define the rooms in your attic, you'll need a sturdy floor beneath it all. Existing floors in most unfinished attics are merely ceiling joists for the floor below and are too small to support a living space.

There are several options for strengthening your attic's floor structure. The simplest method is to install an additional, identically sized joist next to each existing joist, connecting the two with nails. This process is known as *sistering*.

Sistering doesn't work when joists are smaller than 2 × 6s, are spaced too far apart, or where there are obstructions, such as plaster keys, from the ceiling below. An alternative is to build a new floor by placing larger joists between the existing ones. By resting the joists on 2 × 4 spacers, you avoid obstructions and minimize damage to the ceiling surface below. However, be aware that the spacers will reduce your headroom by 1½" inches, plus the added joist depth.

To determine the best option for your attic, consult an architect, engineer, or building contractor, as well as a local building inspector. Ask what size of joists you'll need and which options are allowed in your area. Joist sizing is based on the *span* (the distance between support points), the joist spacing (typically 16" or 24" on-center),

and the type of lumber used. In most cases, an attic floor must be able to support 40 pounds per sq. ft. of *live load* (occupants, furniture) and 10 psf *dead load* (wallboard, floor covering).

The floor joist cavities offer space for concealing the plumbing, wiring, and ductwork servicing your attic, so consider these systems as you plan. You'll also need to locate partition walls to determine if any additional blocking between joists is necessary (see pages 60-61).

When the framing is done, the mechanical elements and insulation are in place, and everything has been inspected and approved, complete the floor by installing ¾" tongue-and-groove plywood. If your remodel will include kneewalls, you can omit the subflooring behind the kneewalls, but there are good reasons not to: A complete subfloor will add strength to the floor, and will provide a sturdy surface for storage.

Everything You Need:

Tools: Circular saw, rafter square, drill, caulk gun.

Materials: 2 × joist lumber; 16d, 10d, and 8d common nails; 2 × 4 lumber, ¾" T&G plywood; construction adhesive; 2¼" wallboard screws.

How to Add Sister Joists

1 Remove all insulation from the joist cavities and carefully remove any blocking or bridging between the joists. Determine the lengths for the sister joists by measuring the existing joists. Also measure at the outside end of each joist to determine how much of the top corner was cut away to fit the joist beneath the roof sheathing. NOTE: Joists that rest on a bearing wall should overlap each other by at least 3".

2 Before cutting, sight down both narrow edges of each board to check for *crowning*—upward arching along the length of the board. Draw an arrow that points in the direction of the arch. Joists must be installed "crown-up;" this arrow designates the top edge. Cut the board to length, then clip the top, outside corner to match the existing joists.

3 Set the sister joists in place, flush against the existing joists and with their ends aligned. Toenail each sister joist to the top plates of both supporting walls, using two 16d common nails.

4 Nail the joists together using 10d common nails. Drive three nails in a row, spacing the rows 12" to 16" apart. To minimize damage to the ceiling surface below caused by the hammering (such as cracking and nail popping), you can use an air-powered nail gun (available at rental stores), or 3" lag screws instead of nails. Install new blocking between the sistered joists, as required by the local building code.

How to Build a New Attic Floor

1 Remove any blocking or bridging from between the existing joists, being careful not to disturb the ceiling below. Cut 2 × 4 spacers to fit snugly between each pair of joists. Lay the spacers flat against the top plate of all supporting walls, and nail them in place with 16d common nails.

2 Create a layout for the new joists by measuring across the tops of the existing joists and using a rafter square to transfer the measurements down to the spacers. Following 16"-on-center spacing, mark the layout along one exterior wall, then mark an identical layout onto the interior bearing wall. Note that the layout on the opposing exterior wall will be offset 1½", to account for the joist overlap at the interior wall.

3 To determine joist length, measure from the outer edge of the exterior wall to the far edge of the interior bearing wall. The joists must overlap each other above the interior wall by 3". Before cutting, mark the top edge of each joist (see step 2, page 49). Cut the joists to length, then clip the top, outside corners so the ends can fit under the roof sheathing.

4 Set the joists in place on their layout marks. Toenail the outside end of each joist to the spacer on the exterior wall, using three 8d common nails.

5 Nail the joists together where they overlap atop the interior bearing wall, using three 10d nails for each. Toenail the joists to the spacers on the interior bearing wall, using 8d nails.

6 Install blocking or bridging between the joists, as required by the local building code. As a suggested minimum, the new joists should be blocked as close as possible to the outside ends and where they overlap at the interior wall.

How to Install Subflooring

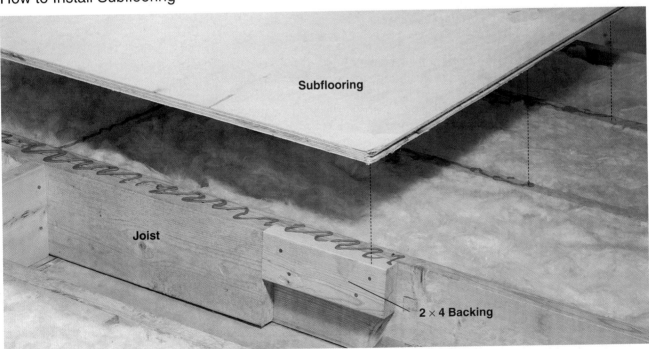

Subflooring

Joist

2 × 4 Backing

Install the subflooring only after all framing, plumbing, wiring, and ductwork is completed and has received the required building inspections. Also install any insulation and complete any caulking necessary for soundproofing (see pages 102-103). Follow steps 6-8 on page 47 for the general subflooring procedure. Fasten the sheets with construction adhesive and 2¼" wallboard or deck screws, making sure the sheets are perpendicular to the joists and the end joints are staggered between rows. Where joists overlap at an interior bearing wall, add backing as needed to compensate for the offset in the layout. Nail a 2 × 4 or wider board to the face of each joist to support the edges of the intervening sheets.

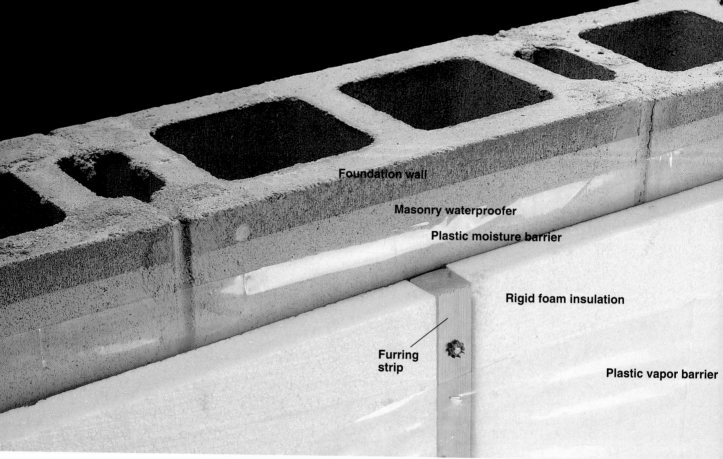

Foundation wall

Masonry waterproofer

Plastic moisture barrier

Rigid foam insulation

Furring strip

Plastic vapor barrier

Local building codes may require a barrier to prevent moisture from damaging wood and insulation covering foundation walls. This may be masonry waterproofer, or plastic sheeting placed behind or in front of the framing.

Covering Foundation Walls

There are two common methods for covering foundation walls. Because it saves space, the more popular method is to attach 2 × 2 furring strips directly to the masonry wall. These strips provide a 1½"-deep cavity between strips for insulation and service lines, as well as a framework for attaching wallboard. The other method is to build a complete 2 × 4 stud wall just in front of the foundation wall. This method offers a full 3½" for insulation and lines, and it provides a flat, plumb wall surface, regardless of the foundation wall's condition.

To determine the best method for your project, examine the foundation walls. If they're fairly plumb and flat, you can consider furring them. If the walls are wavy or out of plumb, however, it may be easier to build stud walls. Also check with the local building department before you decide on a framing method. There may be codes regarding insulation minimums and methods of running service lines along foundation walls.

A local building official can also tell you what's recommended—or required—in your area for sealing foundation walls against moisture. Com-

mon types of moisture barriers include masonry waterproofers that are applied like paint and plastic sheeting installed between masonry walls and wood framing. The local building code will also specify whether you need a vapor barrier between the framing and the wallboard (see pages 98-99).

Before you shop for materials, decide how you'll fasten the wood framing to your foundation walls and floor. The three most common methods are shown on pages 53-54. If you're covering a large wall area, it will be worth it to buy or rent a powder-actuated nailer for the job.

Everything You Need:

Tools: Caulk gun, trowel, paint roller, circular saw, drill, powder-actuated nailer, plumb bob.

Materials: Paper-faced insulation, silicone caulk, hydraulic cement, masonry waterproofer, 2 × 2 and 2 × 4 lumber, 2½" wallboard screws, construction adhesive, concrete fasteners, insulation.

How to Seal and Prepare Masonry Walls

Insulate the rim-joist cavities (above the foundation walls) with solid pieces of paper-faced fiberglass insulation. Make sure the paper, which serves as a vapor barrier, faces the room. Also apply silicone caulk to the joints between the sill plates and the foundation walls (inset).

Fill small cracks with hydraulic cement or masonry caulk, and smooth the excess with a trowel. Ask the building department whether masonry waterproofer or a plastic moisture barrier is required in your area. Apply waterproofer as directed by the manufacturer, or install plastic sheeting following code specifications.

Options for Attaching Wood to Masonry

Masonry nails are the cheapest way to attach wood to concrete block walls. Drive the nails into the mortar joints for maximum holding power and to avoid cracking the blocks. Drill pilot holes through the strips if the nails cause splitting. Masonry nails are difficult to drive into poured concrete.

Self-tapping masonry screws hold well in block or poured concrete, but they must be driven into predrilled holes. Use a hammer drill to drill holes of the same size in both the wood and the concrete after the wood is positioned. Drive the screws into the *web* portion of the blocks (see page 54).

(continued next page)

Options for Attaching Wood to Masonry (continued)

Webs

Powder-actuated nailers offer the quickest and easiest method for fastening framing to block, poured concrete, and steel. They use individual caps of gunpowder—called *loads*—to propel a piston that drives a hardened-steel nail (*pin*) through the wood and into the masonry. The loads are color-coded for the charge they produce, and the pins come in various lengths. Note: Always drive pins into the solid web portions of concrete blocks, not into the voids.

Trigger-type nailers, like the one shown here, are easiest to use, but hammer-activated types are also available. You can buy nailers at home centers and hardware stores, or rent them from rental centers. (Ask for a demonstration at the rental center.) Always wear hearing and eye protection when using these extremely loud tools.

How to Install Furring Strips on Masonry Walls

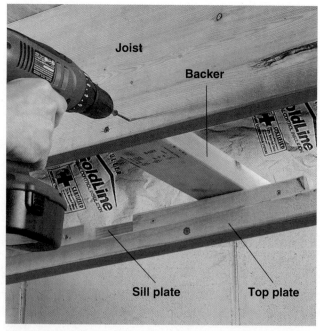

Joist

Backer

Sill plate

Top plate

1 Cut a 2 × 2 top plate to span the length of the wall. Mark the furring-strip layout onto the bottom edge of the plate, using 16"-on-center spacing (see step 2, page 61). Attach the plate to the bottom of the joists with 2½" wallboard screws. The back edge of the plate should line up with the front of the blocks.

NOTE: If the joists run parallel to the wall, you'll need to install backers between the outer joist and the sill plate to provide support for ceiling wallboard. Make T-shaped backers from short 2 × 4s and 2 × 2s. Install each so the bottom face of the 2 × 4 is flush with the bottom edge of the joists. Attach the top plate to the foundation wall with its top edge flush with the top of the blocks.

54

2 Install a bottom plate cut from pressure-treated 2 × 2 lumber so the plate spans the length of the wall. Apply construction adhesive to the back and bottom of the plate, then attach it to the floor with a nailer. Use a plumb bob to transfer the furring-strip layout marks from the top plate to the bottom plate.

3 Cut 2 × 2 furring strips to fit between the top and bottom plates. Apply construction adhesive to the back of each furring strip, and position it on the layout marks on the plates. Nail along the length of each strip at 16" intervals.

Option: Leave a channel for the installation of wires or supply pipes by installing pairs of vertically aligned furring strips with a 2" gap between each pair. NOTE: Consult local codes to ensure proper installation of electrical or plumbing materials.

4 Fill the cavities between furring strips with rigid insulation board. Cut the pieces so they fit snugly within the framing. If necessary, make cutouts in the insulation to fit around mechanical elements, and cover any channels with metal protective plates before attaching the wall surface. Add a vapor barrier if required by local building code (see pages 98-99).

Tips for Covering Foundation Walls with Stud Walls

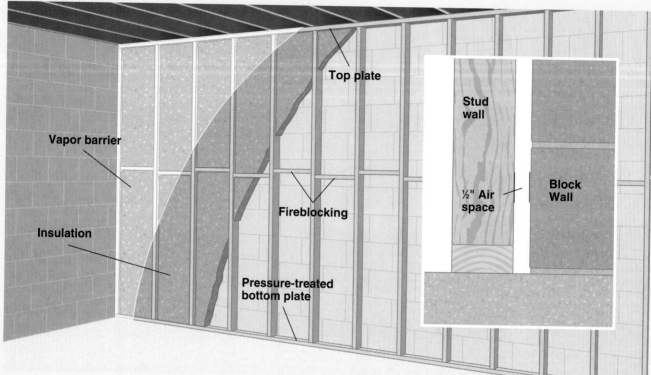

Build a standard 2 × 4 partition wall, following the basic steps on pages 60-63. Use pressure-treated lumber for any bottom plates that rest on concrete. To minimize moisture problems and avoid unevenness in foundation walls, leave a ½" air space between the stud walls and the masonry walls (inset). Insulate the stud walls with fiberglass blankets, and install a vapor barrier if required by local code. Also install all fireblocking required by local code.

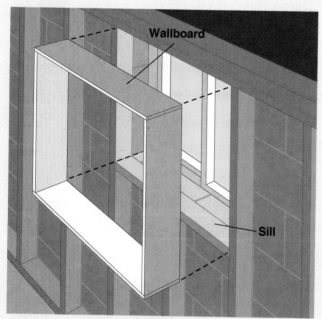

Frame around a basement window so the framing is flush with the edges of the masonry on all sides. Install a sill at the base of the window opening, and add a header, if necessary. Fill the space between the framing members and the masonry with fiberglass insulation or non-expanding foam insulation. Install wallboard so it butts against the window frame.

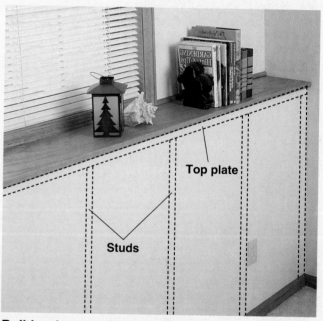

Build a short stud wall to cover a low foundation wall in a walkout or "daylight" basement. Install the top plate flush with the top of the foundation wall. Finish the wall surface with wallboard or other finish, then cap the walls with finish-grade lumber or plywood to create a decorative shelf.

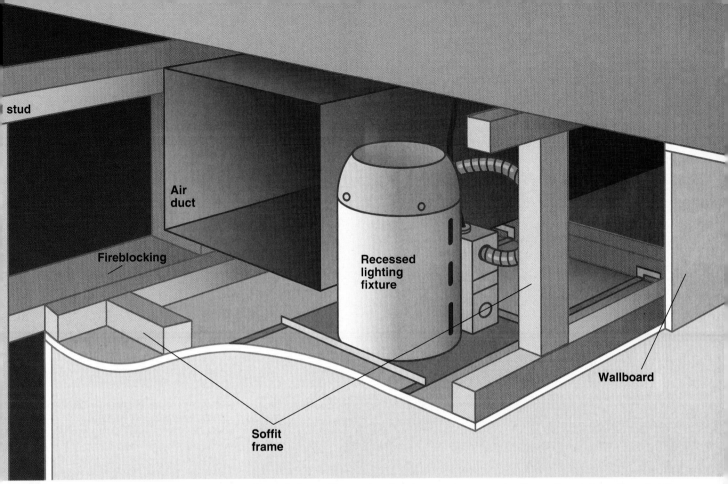

Air
duct

Fireblocking

Recessed
lighting
fixture

Wallboard

Soffit
frame

Hide immovable obstructions in a soffit built from dimension lumber and covered with wallboard or other finish material. An extra-wide soffit is also a great place to install recessed lighting fixtures.

Framing Soffits & Chases

Your unfinished basement or attic is sure to have beams, pipes, posts, ductwork, and other elements that are vital to your house but become big obstacles to finishing the space. When you can't conceal the obstructions within walls, and you've determined it's too costly to move them, hide them inside a framed soffit or chase. This can also provide a place to run smaller mechanicals, like wiring and water supply lines.

Soffits and chases are easy to build. A soffit is usually constructed with 2 × 2 lumber, which is easy to work with and inexpensive. You can use 1 × 3s to keep the frame as small as possible and 2 × 4s for large soffits that will house other elements, such as lighting fixtures. Chases should be framed with 2 × 4s.

This section shows you some basic techniques for building soffits and chases, but the design of your framing is up to you. For example, you may want to shape your soffits for a decorative effect, or build an oversize chase that holds bookshelves. Just make sure the framing conforms to

local building codes. There may be code restrictions about the types of mechanicals that can be grouped together, as well as minimum clearances between the framing and what it encloses. And most codes specify that soffits, chases, and other framed structures have fireblocking every 10 ft. and at the intersections between soffits and neighboring walls. Remember, too, that drain cleanouts and shutoff valves must be accessible, so you'll need to install access panels at these locations.

Everything You Need:

Tools: Circular saw, drill, powder-actuated nailer.

Materials: Standard lumber (1 × 3, 2 × 2, 2 × 4), pressure-treated 2 × 4s, construction adhesive, wallboard, unfaced fiberglass insulation, nails, wood trim, plywood, wallboard screws, decorative screws.

Variations for Building Soffits

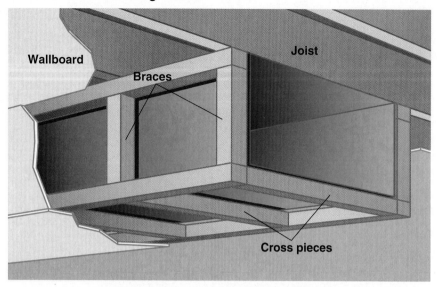

Wallboard

Braces

Joist

Cross pieces

Obstructions perpendicular to joists. Build two ladder-like frames for the soffit sides, using standard 2 × 2s. Install 2 × 2 braces (or "rungs") every 16" or 24" to provide nailing support for the edges of the wallboard or other finish material. Attach the side frames to the joists on either side of the obstruction, using nails or screws. Then, install cross pieces beneath the obstacle, tying the two sides together. Cover the soffit with wallboard, plywood, or other finish material.

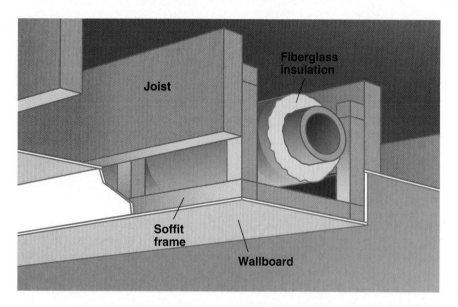

Joist

Fiberglass insulation

Soffit frame

Wallboard

Obstructions parallel to joists. Build side frames as with perpendicular obstructions, but size them to fit in between two joists. This provides nailing surfaces for both the soffit and ceiling finish materials. Attach the frames to the joists with screws, then install cross pieces. NOTE: If you are enclosing a drain pipe, wrap the pipe in unfaced fiberglass insulation to muffle the sound of draining water.

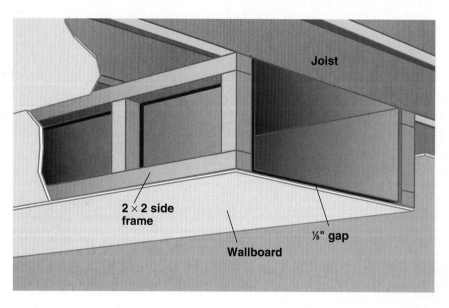

Joist

2 × 2 side frame

⅛" gap

Wallboard

Maximize headroom. In rooms with low ceilings, and where an obstruction is less than 12" wide and the finish material will be wallboard or plywood, build side frames (see above) so that the bottom edges are ⅛" lower than the lowest point of the obstruction. For soffits of this width, the bottom piece of wallboard or plywood stabilizes the structure, so cross pieces between side frames aren't necessary.

How to Frame a Chase

Build chases with 2 × 4s, which tend to be straighter than 2 × 2s and are strong enough to withstand household accidents. Use pressure-treated lumber for bottom plates on concrete floors, attaching them with construction adhesive and powder-actuated nailer fasteners (see page 54). Cut top plates from standard lumber and nail or screw them in place. Install studs to form the corners of the chase, and block in between them for stability. To make the chase smaller, notch the top and bottom plates around the obstruction, and install the studs flat. If you're framing around a vertical drain pipe (especially the main DWV stack), leave room around the pipe for soundproofing insulation; plastic pipes can be especially noisy.

How to Make Access Panels

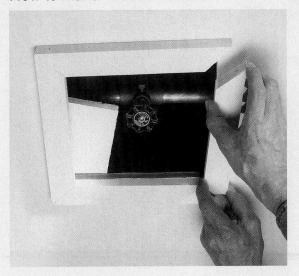

Plywood backer strip

After your soffits and chases are framed, note the locations of all access points before you install the wallboard. Make the access panels after the wallboard is installed.

In a horizontal surface (top photo), cut out a square piece of wallboard at the access location. Push the cutout through the opening and slide it to one side so it rests on the inside of the soffit. Glue mitered trim around the opening so it over-laps the opening by approximately ½" on all sides. Position the panel so it rests on the trim and can be moved when necessary.

In a vertical surface (bottom photo), cut an opening in the same fashion, and glue mitered trim to the edges of the cutout to create the panel. Install plywood backer strips to the back of the wallboard at two sides of the opening. Position the finished panel over the opening so it rests against the strips. Drill pilot holes through the trim, and secure the panel to the backer strips with decorative screws.

Wall
studs

Top plate

Cripple
stud

Header

King
stud

Jack
stud

Bottom
plate

A typical partition wall consists of top and bottom plates and 2 × 4 studs spaced 16" on center. Use 2 × 6 lumber for walls that will hold large plumbing pipes (inset).

Building Partition Walls

Non-load-bearing, or partition, walls are typically built with 2 × 4 lumber and are supported by ceiling or floor joists above or by blocking between the joists. For basement walls that sit on bare concrete, use pressure-treated lumber for the bottom plates.

This project shows you how to build a wall in place, rather than how to build a complete wall on the floor and tilt it upright, as in new construction. The build-in-place method allows for variations in floor and ceiling levels and is generally much easier for remodeling projects.

If your wall will include a door or other opening, see pages 68-71 before laying out the wall. NOTE: After your walls are framed and the mechanical rough-ins are completed, be sure to install metal protector plates where pipes and wires run through framing members (see page 104).

Everything You Need:

Tools: Chalk line, circular saw, framing square, plumb bob, powder-actuated nailer, T-bevel.

Materials: 2 × 4 lumber, blocking lumber, 16d and 8d common nails, concrete fasteners, wallboard screws.

Variations for Fastening Top Plates to Joists

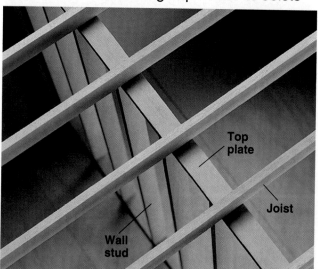

Top
plate

Joist

Wall
stud

When a new wall is perpendicular to the ceiling or floor joists above, attach the top plate directly to the joists, using 16d nails.

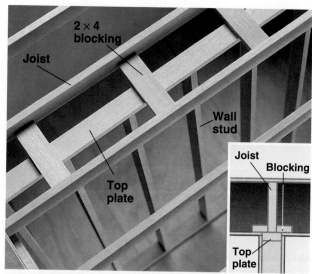

2 × 4
blocking

Joist

Wall
stud

Top
plate

Joist

Blocking

Top
plate

When a new wall falls between parallel joists, install 2 × 4 blocking between the joists every 24". The blocking supports the new wall's top plate and provides backing for the ceiling wallboard. If the new wall is aligned with a parallel joist, install blocks on both sides of the wall, and attach the top plate to the joist (inset).

Variations for Fastening Bottom Plates to Joists

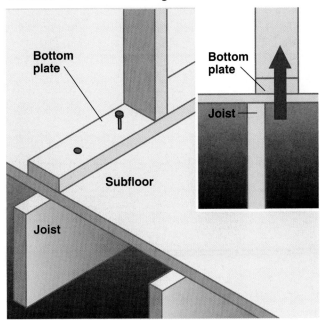

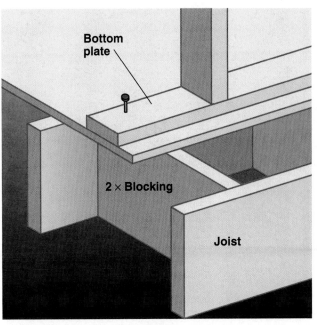

If a new wall is aligned with a joist below, install the bottom plate directly over the joist or off-center over the joist (inset). Off-center placement allows you to nail into the joist but provides room underneath the plate for pipes or wiring to go up into the wall.

If a new wall falls between parallel joists, install 2 × 6 or larger blocking between the two joists below, spaced 24" on center. Nail the bottom plate through the subfloor and into the blocking.

How to Build a Partition Wall

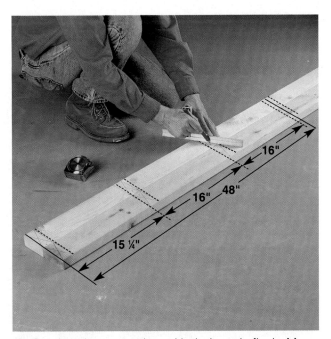

1 Mark the location of the leading edge of the new wall's top plate, then snap a chalk line through the marks across the joists or blocks. Use a framing square, or take measurements, to make sure the line is perpendicular to any intersecting walls. Cut the top and bottom plates to length.

2 Set the plates together with their ends flush. Measure from the end of one plate, and make marks for the location of each stud. The first stud should fall 15¼" from the end; every stud thereafter should fall 16" on center. Thus, the first 4 × 8-ft. wallboard panel will cover the first stud and "break" in the center of the fourth stud. Use a square to extend the marks across both plates. Draw an "X" at each stud location.

(continued next page)

How to Build a Partition Wall (continued)

3 Position the top plate against the joists, aligning its leading edge with the chalk line. Attach the plate with two 16d nails driven into each joist. Start at one end, and adjust the plate as you go to keep the leading edge flush with the chalk line.

4 To position the bottom plate, hang a plumb bob from the side edge of the top plate so the point nearly touches the floor. When it hangs motionless, mark the point's location on the floor. Make plumb markings at each end of the top plate, then snap a chalk line between the marks. Position the bottom plate along the chalk line, and use the plumb bob to align the the stud markings between the two plates.

5 Fasten the bottom plate to the floor. On concrete, use a powder-actuated nailer or masonry screws (see pages 53-54), driving a pin or screw every 16". On wood floors, use 16d nails driven into the joists or sleepers below.

6 Measure between the plates for the length of each stud. Cut each stud so it fits snugly in place but is not so tight that it bows the joists above. If you cut a stud too short, see if it will fit somewhere else down the wall.

7 Install the studs by toenailing them at a 60° angle through the sides of the studs and into the plates. At each end, drive two 8d nails through one side of the stud and one more through the center on the other side.

How to Frame Corners (shown in cutaways)

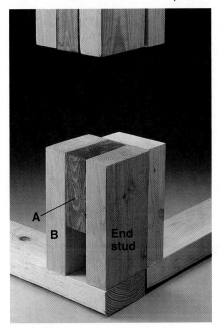  

L-corners: Nail 2 × 4 spacers (A) to the inside of the end stud. Nail an extra stud (B) to the spacers. The extra stud provides a surface to attach wallboard at the inside corner.

T-corner meets stud: Fasten 2 × 2 backers (A) to each side of the side-wall stud (B). The backers provide a nailing surface for wallboard.

T-corner between studs: Fasten a 1 × 6 backer (A) to the end stud (B) with wallboard screws. The backer provides a nailing surface for wallboard.

How to Frame an Angled Partition Wall in an Attic

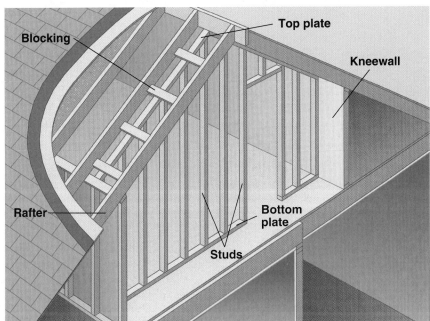 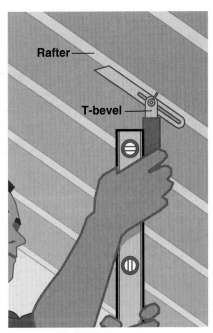

Full-size attic partition walls typically run parallel to the rafters and have sloping top plates that extend down to knee walls on either side. To build one, cut the top and bottom plates, and mark the stud locations on the bottom plate only. Nail the top plates in place, and use a plumb bob to position the bottom plate, as with a standard wall. Use the plumb bob again to transfer the stud layout marks from the bottom to the top plate. To find the proper angle for cutting the top ends of the studs, set a level against the top plate (or rafter) and hold it plumb. Then, rest the handle of a T-bevel against the level, and adjust the T-bevel blade to follow the plate. Transfer the angle to the stud ends, and cut them to length.

Building Attic Kneewalls

Attic kneewalls are short walls that extend from the attic floor to the rafters. They provide a vertical dimension to attic rooms, and without them, attics tend to feel cramped. Kneewalls are typically 5 ft. tall, for a couple of reasons: That's the minimum ceiling height for usable floor space according to most building codes, and it defines a comfortable room without wasting too much floor space. The unfinished space behind kneewalls doesn't have to go to waste: It's great for storage and for concealing service lines. To provide access to this space, create a framed opening in the wall during the framing process (see pages 68-70).

Kneewalls are similar to partition walls, except they have beveled top plates and angle-cut studs that follow the slope of the rafters. The added stud depth created by the angled cut requires a 2 × 6 top plate. Before starting on your kneewall project, it may help to review the techniques for building a partition wall (pages 60-63).

> **Everything You Need:**
>
> Tools: Circular saw, level, chalk line, T-bevel.
>
> Materials: 2 × 4 and 2 × 6 lumber, 16d and 8d common nails.

Attic kneewalls are just the right height to be backdrops for furniture, and they make a perfect foundation for built-in storage units (see pages 146-149).

How to Build a Kneewall

1 Create a storyboard using a straight 2 × 4. Cut the board a few inches longer than the planned height of the wall. Measure from one end and draw a line across the front edge of the board at the exact wall height.

2 At one end of the room, set the storyboard flat against the outer rafter. Plumb the storyboard with a level while aligning the height mark with the bottom edge of the rafter. Transfer the height mark onto the rafter edge, then make a mark along the front edge of the storyboard onto the subfloor. These marks represent the top and bottom wall plates.

3 Holding the storyboard perfectly plumb, trace along the bottom edge of the rafter to transfer the rafter slope onto the face of the storyboard.

4 Repeat the wall-plate marking process on the other end of the room. Snap a chalk line through the marks—across the rafters and along the subfloor. If necessary, add backing for fastening the top plate to the gable wall.

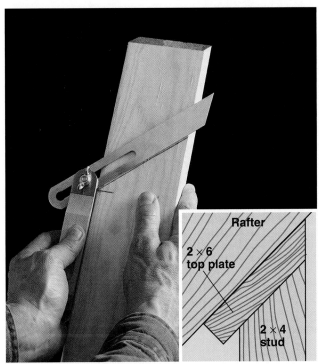

Rafter

2 × 6 top plate

2 × 4 stud

5 To cut a beveled edge on the top wall plate, set a T-bevel to match the rafter-slope line on the storyboard. Use the T-bevel to adjust the blade of a circular saw or table saw to the proper angle. Then, bevel-cut one edge of the 2 × 6 top plate. NOTE: When the top plate is laid flat across the rafters, the front edge should be perpendicular to the floor (inset).

6 Mark the stud locations on the wall plates (see pages 61-62). Install the plates along the chalk lines, fastening them to the rafters and floor joists, respectively, using 16d nails. Measure and cut each stud to fit, angle-cutting the top end so that it meets flush with the top plate. Toenail each stud in place with three 8d nails.

Framing an Attic Ceiling

By virtue of sloping roofs, most attics naturally have "cathedral" ceilings. It's up to you whether to leave the peaks intact—and apply a finish surface all the way up to the ridge—or to frame-in a horizontal ceiling, creating a flat surface that's more like a standard ceiling. Before deciding, consider the advantages and disadvantages of each treatment.

If your attic has collar ties—horizontal braces installed between opposing rafters—your planning should start with those. Are the ties high enough to meet the code requirements for attic headroom? If not, consult an architect or engineer to see if you can move them up a few inches (do not move or remove them without professional guidance). If the ties are high enough, you can incorporate them into a new ceiling or leave them exposed and wrap them with a finish material, such as wallboard or finish-grade lumber. Do not use collar ties as part of your ceiling frame.

A peaked ceiling is primarily an aesthetic option. Its height expands the visual space of the room, and its rising angles provide a dramatic look that's unique in most homes. Because a peaked ceiling encloses the rafter bays all the way up to the ridge, this treatment may require additional roof vents to maintain proper ventilation (see pages 100-101).

By contrast, a flat ceiling typically offers a cleaner, more finished appearance closer to that of a conventional room, and flat ceilings offer some practical advantages over peaked styles. First, they provide a concealed space above the ceiling, great for running service lines. If there are vents high on the gable walls, this open space can help ventilate the roof (make sure to insulate above the ceiling). The ceiling itself can hold recessed lighting fixtures or support a ceiling fan. And if your plans call for full-height partition walls, you may want a ceiling frame to enclose the top of the wall.

When determining the height of flat-ceiling framing, be sure to account for the floor and ceiling finishes. And remember that most building codes require a finished ceiling height of at least 90".

Everything You Need:

Tools: 4-ft. level, chalk line, circular saw.

Materials: 2 × 4 and 2 × 6 lumber, 10d common nails.

Flat attic ceilings provide space for recessed light fixtures, vents, and speakers.

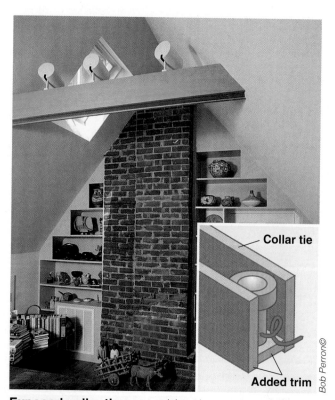

Bob Perron©

Exposed collar ties can add an interesting architectural element to a peaked ceiling. By adding to the existing ties, you can create a channel for holding small light fixtures (inset).

Collar tie

Added trim

How to Frame a Flat Ceiling

1 Make a storyboard for the planned height of the ceiling frame (see step 1, page 64). At one end of the attic, hold the storyboard plumb and align the height mark with the bottom edge of a rafter. Transfer the mark to the rafter. Repeat at the other end of the attic, then snap a chalk line through the marks. This line represents the bottom edge of the ceiling frame.

2 Using a level and the storyboard, level over from the chalk line and mark two outside rafters on the other side of the attic. Snap a chalk line through the marks. NOTE: The storyboard is used merely as a straightedge for this step.

3 Cut 2 × 6 joists to span across the rafters, angle-cutting the ends to follow the roof pitch. Check each joist for crowning to make sure you're cutting it so it will be installed with the crowned edge up (see step 2, page 49). Make the overall length about ½" short so the ends of the joists won't touch the roof sheathing.

4 Nail each joist to the rafters with three 10d common nails at each end. Be sure to maintain 16"- or 24"-on-center spacing between joists to provide support for attaching wallboard or other finish material.

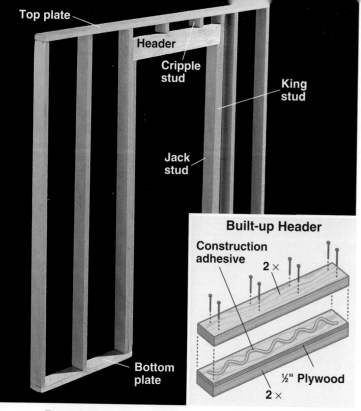

Labels on top image:
Top plate, Header, Cripple stud, King stud, Jack stud

Built-up Header
Construction adhesive
2 ×
½" Plywood
2 ×
Bottom plate

Door frames for prehung doors start with *king* studs that attach to the top and bottom plates. Inside the king studs, *jack* studs support the *header* at the top of the opening. *Cripple* studs continue the wall-stud layout above the opening. In non-load-bearing walls, the header may be a 2 × 4 laid flat or a built-up header (inset). The dimensions of the framed opening are referred to as the *rough opening*.

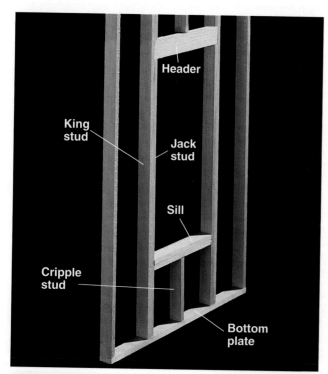

Labels on bottom image:
Header, King stud, Jack stud, Sill, Cripple stud, Bottom plate

Window frames, like door frames, have full-length king studs, as well as jack studs that support the header. They also have a *sill* that defines the bottom of the rough opening.

Framing Doors & Windows

In new walls, build your door frames along with the rest of the wall. The project shown here demonstrates framing a rough opening for an interior prehung door in a new, non-load-bearing partition wall. The basic steps are the same for closet doors. However, for large closet openings, such as for double bi-fold or by-pass doors, use a built-up header: two 2 × 4s set on edge and nailed together with a strip of ½"-thick plywood in between. This provides additional strength to support the weight of the doors.

Although most windows in a house are located in load-bearing exterior walls, standard attic windows are commonly located in gable walls, which often are non-load-bearing. Installing a window in a non-load-bearing gable wall is fairly simple and doesn't require temporary support for the framing. Some gable walls, however, are load-bearing: A common sign is a heavy structural ridge beam that supports the rafters from underneath, rather than merely at the rafter ends. Hire a contractor to build window frames in load-bearing gable walls. If you aren't certain what type of wall you have, consult a professional.

A common problem with framing in a gable wall is that the positions of the floor joists may make it difficult to attach new studs to the bottom wall plate. One solution is to install an extra-long header and sill between two existing studs, positioning them at the precise heights for the rough opening. You can then adjust the width of the rough opening by installing vertical studs between the header and sill.

When planning the placement of attic windows, remember that the bottom of an egress window must be no higher than 44" from the finished floor (see page 16). Windows lower than 24" may require tempered glazing.

To lay out and build a door or window frame, you'll need the actual dimensions of the door or window unit, so it's best to have the unit on hand for the framing process.

Everything You Need:

Tools: Circular saw, handsaw, plumb bob, T-bevel, 4-ft. level, combination square, reciprocating saw.

Materials: Framed door or window unit; 2 × 4 lumber; 16d, 10d, and 8d common nails; ½"-thick plywood; construction adhesive.

How to Frame a Rough Opening for an Interior Prehung Door

King stud marking

King stud marking

Door unit width

Extra ½"

Extra ½"

Jack stud marking

Jack stud marking

1 To mark the layout for the studs that make up the door frame, measure the width of the door unit along the bottom. Add 1" to this dimension to calculate the width of the rough opening (the distance between the jack studs). This gives you a ½" gap on each side for adjusting the door frame during installation. Mark the top and bottom plates for the jack and king studs.

2 After you've installed the wall plates (see pages 60-63), cut the king studs and toenail them in place at the appropriate markings.

3 Measure the full length of the door unit, then add ½" to determine the height of the rough opening. Using that dimension, measure up from the floor and mark the king studs. Cut a 2 × 4 header to fit between the king studs. Position the header flat, with its bottom face at the marks, and secure it to the king studs with 16d nails.

4 Cut and install a cripple stud above the header, centered between the king studs. Install any additional cripples required to maintain the 16"-on-center layout of the standard studs in the rest of the wall.

(continued next page)

How to Frame a Rough Opening for an Interior Prehung Door (continued)

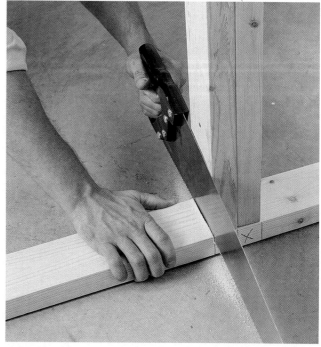

5 Cut the jack studs to fit snugly under the header. Fasten them in place by nailing down through the header, then drive 10d nails through the faces of the jack studs and into the king studs, spaced 16" apart.

6 Saw through the bottom plate so it's flush with the inside faces of the jack studs. Remove the cut-out portion of the plate. NOTE: If the wall will be finished with wallboard, hang the door after the wallboard is installed.

How to Frame a Window Opening in a Gable Wall (non-load-bearing)

1 Determine the rough opening width by measuring the window unit and adding 1". Add 3" to that dimension to get the distance between the king studs. Mark the locations of the king studs onto the bottom plate of the gable wall.

2 Using a plumb bob, transfer the king-stud marks from the bottom plate to the sloping top plates of the gable wall.

3 Cut the king studs to length, angle-cutting the top ends so they meet flush with the top plates (see page 63). Fasten each king stud in place by toenailing the ends with three 8d nails.

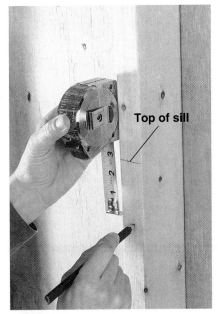

4 Find the height of the rough opening by measuring the height of the window unit and adding ½". Measure up from where the finished floor height will be, and mark the top of the sill. Make a second mark for the bottom of the sill, 3" down from the top mark.

Top of sill

5 Measure up from the top sill mark, and mark the height of the rough opening (bottom of header). Make another mark 3½" up, to indicate the top of the header. Using a level, transfer all of these marks to the other king stud and to all intermediate studs.

6 Draw level cutting lines across the intermediate studs at the marks for the bottom of the sill and top of the header. Cut along the lines with a reciprocating saw, then remove the cut-out portions. The remaining stud sections will serve as cripple studs.

7 Cut the jack studs to reach from the bottom plate to the bottom header marks on the king studs. Nail the jack studs to the inside faces of the king studs using 10d common nails driven every 16".

8 Build a built-up header with 2 × 4s and plywood (see page 68). Size the header to fit snugly between the king studs. Set the header on top of the jack studs. Nail through the king studs into the header with 16d nails, then toenail the jack studs and cripple studs to the header, using 8d nails.

9 Build the sill to fit snugly between the jack studs by nailing together two 2 × 4s. Position the sill at the top sill markings, and toenail it to the jack studs. Toenail the cripple studs to the sill. See pages 122-125 to learn how to remove the exterior wall finish and install the window.

Basement window openings must have support above to carry the weight of the house. An opening in masonry is usually fitted with wood bucks to serve as a rough window frame.

Photo courtesy of The Bilco Company

Egress windows in basements require large wells that meet code specifications (see page 75). The prefabricated window well shown here has a stepped side that serves as stairs for emergency escape. Spaces behind the steps can hold plants to dress up the view from the window.

Enlarging a Basement Window Opening

Whether the goal is to add more natural light or to provide emergency egress, enlarging a window opening for a new window is a common project for basement remodels. However, it's not always a do-it-yourself job. There are many factors to consider, and depending on your basement configuration and the size of window you want, it may be best to hire a professional to do some or all of the work. If you want to add a window where none already exists, have a professional create the new opening for you.

The first, and most important, consideration is ensuring there will be adequate support for your house once the window opening is expanded or created. If you're not changing the width of the opening, the means for support should already be in place. Increasing the opening's width, however, will require a new wood header or a steel lintel to span the top of the opening and carry the weight from above.

The second consideration is the window well, which must be dug before the window can be expanded. Digging a window well can be a fairly extensive project; the discussion of window wells on page 75 gives you an idea of what's involved.

After preparing the well comes the task of cutting into the foundation wall. With concrete block, this is a messy job but surprisingly easy. The major steps for removing concrete block are shown on pages 73-74. If your foundation walls are poured concrete, you'll need to have a professional cut the opening. For many window types, the rough opening in the masonry must be wrapped with dimension lumber to provide a frame for fastening the window. The lumber pieces—called *bucks*—are usually 2 × 10s or 2 × 12s and should cover the width of the block. To prevent rotting from moisture, use pressure-treated lumber for the window bucks.

Everything You Need:

Tools: Level, masonry chisel, hand maul, circular saw, masonry saw blade, masonry hammer, trowel, drill, hammer drill, masonry bit, caulk gun.

Materials: Concrete, construction adhesive, pressure-treated 2 × lumber, self-tapping masonry screws, silicone caulk.

How to Enlarge a Window Opening in a Concrete Block Wall

1 Remove the old window unit and frame, then mark the rough opening on both the interior and exterior surfaces of the wall, using a level as a guide.

2 Score the cutting lines, using a masonry chisel and hand maul. Be sure to wear eye protection and work gloves.

3 Cut along the scored lines with a circular saw and masonry blade. Make several passes with the saw, gradually deepening the cut until the saw blade is at maximum depth.

4 Break both the inside and outside mortar lines on all sides of the center block in the top row of the area being removed.

(continued next page)

5 Strike the face of the center block with a masonry hammer until the block either comes loose or breaks into pieces.

6 Chip out large pieces, then break the mortar around the remaining blocks. Chip out the remaining blocks using the chisel and maul.

7 Create a smooth surface by filling the hollow areas in the cut blocks with broken pieces of concrete block, then troweling in fresh concrete. Make sure all of the surfaces are flat. Let the concrete dry overnight.

8 Cut pressure-treated 2 × lumber to frame the opening. If necessary, rip-cut the bucks to width so they are flush with the block on both sides. Apply construction adhesive to the bucks and set them in place.

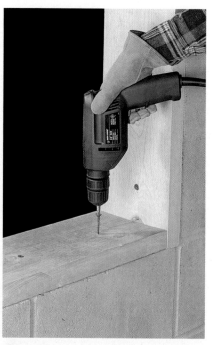

9 Anchor the bucks by drilling pilot holes with a masonry bit, then driving self-tapping masonry screws (see page 53) into the blocks, spaced every 10". Seal the joints between the bucks and the masonry with silicone caulk—on both sides of the wall.

Window Wells

Window wells for standard basement windows are usually small steel shells that let in very little natural light. If your basement project includes expanding existing window openings or adding new ones, you'll need wells that make the most of the new windows. If you're adding an egress window (see page 16) for a bedroom or as a secondary fire escape, the window well must be built to strict building code specifications. There are also some general considerations for wells, such as appearance, size, and drainage.

Window wells can be made of a variety of different materials. Prefabricated wells include the standard corrugated steel type that you can buy at home centers and specialty units made of polyethylene (see page 72). For a custom-built well, you can use concrete block, landscaping timbers, and boulders.

Sizing for a window well depends on several factors. First, the well must extend far enough from the foundation to accommodate the window's operation. For example, casement windows need more room than sliders. Secondly, the size of the well affects how much light reaches the window. While a bigger well lets in more light than a smaller one, it also creates a larger hole that children or pets can fall into if it is uncovered, and a large well collects more water. As general minimums, a window well should be about 6" wider than the window opening, and should extend at least 18" from the foundation wall. And all wells should extend 8" below the window sill and 4" above grade.

The minimum dimensions for an egress-window well will be determined by your local building code. Typically, wells for egress windows must be at least 9 sq. ft. overall, measure at least 36" in width, and extend 36" from the foundation wall. Wells more than 44" deep must have a permanently attached ladder or a step system that doesn't interfere with the window's operation.

Providing adequate drainage for your window wells is particularly important if you plan to leave them uncovered. All wells should have a layer of gravel that is at least 6" deep and stops 3" below the window frame. Uncovered wells, however, may need a drain pipe or a continuous layer of gravel that leads to the footing drain or other perimeter drain system.

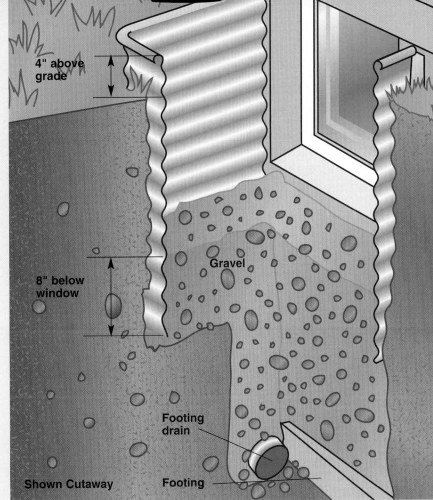

4" above grade

8" below window

Gravel

Footing drain

Shown Cutaway

Footing

Window wells should extend 8" below the window frame and 4" above the ground. Wells for egress windows must be at least 36" wide and project 36" from the foundation, and those deeper than 44" must have a ladder or other means of escape. To keep water from pooling near the window, well bases should have a 6" layer of gravel. More extensive drainage can be provided by gravel that passes water down to a footing drain or by a well drain leading to daylight.

Photo courtesy of The Bilco Company

Plastic well covers keep rain, snow, and debris from entering your well. Covers on egress-window wells must be hinged or easily removable from inside the well.

Systems

Adding the plumbing, wiring, and HVAC (heating, ventilation, and air conditioning) elements is one of the more challenging aspects of basement and attic remodeling. If your current systems can accommodate the added loads, you can expand them by adding new lines to provide service to the space, but making the connections and finding room for everything can be difficult. Finishing a basement means hiding all the mechanical equipment that's already in place, in addition to the new service lines. Attics are simply tough to reach, and providing service often means going through the floors and the walls in between. Considering what's involved, most homeowners seek professional guidance when planning systems expansions for attic or basement conversions.

Before you call a contractor, do some planning on your own. This section can help you get started. There's a discussion of the basic planning steps, followed by some sample projects of popular basement and attic additions. These provide an overview of typical plumbing and wiring installations, including the basic procedures for installing several fixtures. There's also a discussion of your options for heating, cooling, and ventilating your new living space.

After the planning is completed, you may decide to do some of the work yourself. Many homeowners hire professionals to handle the more difficult jobs, like adding circuits and rerouting ductwork, but complete the simpler tasks, like installing fixtures, themselves. If you plan to do your own work, check with the local building department; there may be restrictions on what jobs you can do yourself. And if you're not familiar with any of the procedures involved, make sure you get the help you need—from professionals or reference books—to do the job properly.

Planning Your Systems

Coming up with a plan for your systems involves asking three questions about the finished space: What systems services does each room need? What sources will supply them? and How will these services be delivered? For example, to add a bathroom, determine the plumbing, electrical, heating, and ventilation requirements for the room. Then, examine your home's existing systems to see if they can be expanded to meet these requirements. And finally, find the best way to extend those services to the bathroom. You'll probably have to repeat this process for some of the rooms, so it's best to stay open to alternatives.

To find out what's needed for the room, start by choosing the types of fixtures for the bathroom and making rough plans of the overall room layout. Then consult the local building codes. They will tell you what systems are required, such as a hard-wired vent fan and a permanent light fixture, as well as minimum room dimensions and clearances around fixtures.

When you have a general systems plan for each room, hire the appropriate contractors to assess the plans based on the existing systems in your house. They will check the capacity of each system to determine if it can handle the additional load. For example, if your electrical service panel is nearly full, you may need to install a new subpanel to supply electricity to the new rooms.

The contractors should also help you with the next step: figuring out how to route all the pipes, wires, ducts, etc. to the new rooms. This can be tricky, and you may find it's easier to change a room layout or move a room than to move the needed systems lines. In most cases, locating an attic bathroom over an existing kitchen or bathroom greatly simplifies the plumbing hookups.

Routing the lines themselves often requires creative solutions. Think about the major issues first—ducts and drain pipes are more difficult to route than supply pipes and wiring. You can run many of the lines through and between the framing members of floors, ceilings, and walls. Be sure to follow code restrictions for notching and boring joists and studs, to maintain their structural integrity. When lines can't be hidden within framing, try to group them together so they can be enclosed in a soffit or vertical chase.

Create drawings to work from as you determine the systems necessary for each room.

Check the capacity of your main systems sources to determine if the systems can support additional lines.

Route service lines along walls, joists, and beams so they don't limit headroom in the open area of rooms.

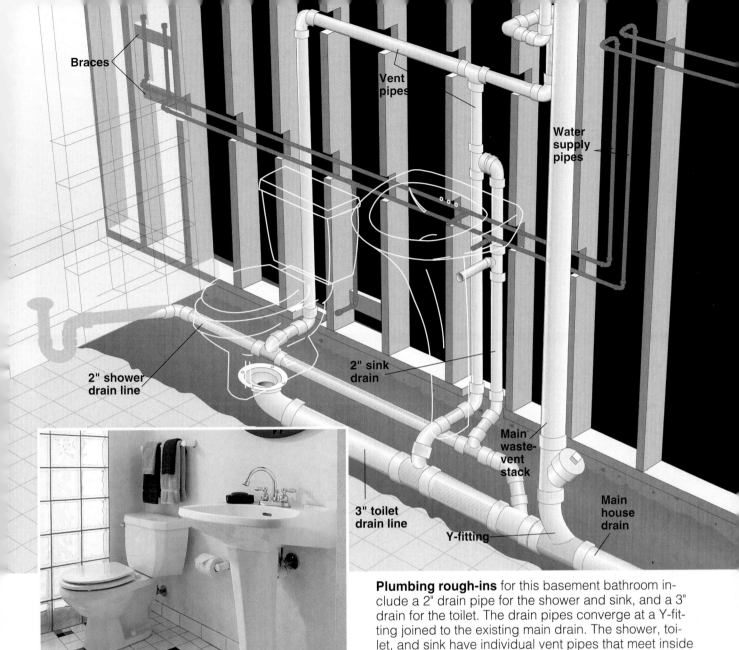

Braces

Vent pipes

Water supply pipes

2" shower drain line

2" sink drain

3" toilet drain line

Y-fitting

Main waste-vent stack

Main house drain

Plumbing rough-ins for this basement bathroom include a 2" drain pipe for the shower and sink, and a 3" drain for the toilet. The drain pipes converge at a Y-fitting joined to the existing main drain. The shower, toilet, and sink have individual vent pipes that meet inside the wet wall. From there, a single vent extends up to the attic, where it joins the main waste-vent stack.

Adding a Basement Bath

Unless your basement has stub-outs in place for adding a bathroom, completing the rough-ins usually requires breaking up a portion of the concrete floor and digging a trench for the toilet and shower or bath drains. To simplify this laborious process, it's best to arrange the bathroom fixtures in a line along one wall. Another consideration is the location of the bathroom: The fixtures must be close enough to the main drain tie-in so that the fixture drain lines maintain a downward slope of ¼" per ft.

In some basements, the main house drain does not extend through the basement floor but instead makes a turn above the floor and begins its run out to the city sewer. In this situation, a basement bathroom requires a *sewage ejector* to collect the waste from each fixture and pump it up to the main drain. Ejectors are available from plumbing dealers, in both under-floor and above-floor models.

The project overview shown here demonstrates the major construction steps of roughing-in a small basement bathroom. The in-floor drains feed into a main drain nearby and are vented by a pipe that ties into the main waste-vent stack in the attic. To accept the new drain tie-ins, the main drain and main waste-vent stack are cut into, and new fittings are added. The project also includes the construction of a 2 × 6 "wet wall" for housing the pipes.

Installation Overview: Basement Bath Plumbing Rough-in

1 Starting 6" from the exterior wall (to leave a ledge for the wet wall), break out a 24"-wide section of concrete. Dig a trench 2" deeper than the main drain.

2 Frame the wet wall, then dry-fit the drain and vent pieces, cutting the pipes to fit. Use supports (inset) to ensure the runs slope downward ¼" per foot.

3 Build a temporary support for the main stack, then cut through the stack and main drain to remove the old fittings. Install the new waste and vent fittings with solvent glue.

4 Glue the drain pieces and test for leaks. Assemble the vent pipes, tying them together in the wall. Run the vent to the attic and connect it to the main stack.

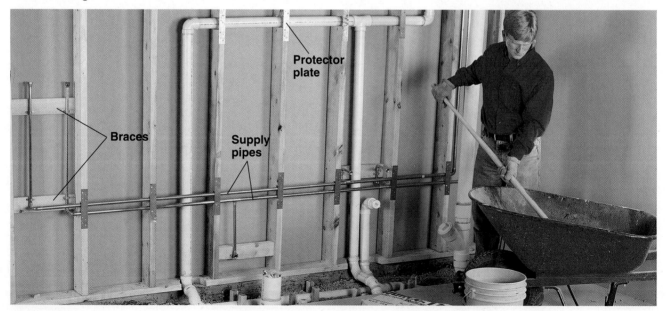

5 Install shutoff valves to the nearest water branch lines, then run ¾" copper lines into the wet wall. Branch off to each fixture with ½" copper pipes. Brace the supply lines, and add protector plates over the stud penetrations. Have everything inspected by a building official before backfilling the trench and pouring new concrete.

Sinks & Vanities

Most vanity tops installed today are integral (one-piece) sink-countertop units made from cultured marble or solid-surface material. These are easy to install and convenient to use, as the sink edge is flush with the countertop. However, you may want to install a laminate or tile countertop with a separate self-rimming or under-mount sink.

When shopping for a bathroom vanity, spend as much as you can afford. Look for quality indicators, like dovetailed or doweled construction, hardwood face frames, doors, and drawer fronts, and a high-gloss, moisture-resistant finish. High-quality cabinetry simply holds up better in humid bathroom environments.

Pre-built vanities are inexpensive and simple to install. Most manufacturers sell additional cabinetry in a matching style. Pedestal sinks (inset) are popular alternatives for smaller bathrooms where floor space is at a premium.

Installation Overview: Vanity & Integral Sink

1 Set the vanity in place. If necessary, add shims so that the unit is plumb and level. Attach the unit to the wall studs with screws.

2 Apply a bead of caulk to the top edge of the vanity, and set the sink-countertop unit into the caulk. Fasten the top following the manufacturer's directions.

3 Install the faucet and drain tailpiece. Complete the drain hookup with a P-trap and trap arm, then connect the water supply tubes to the faucet tailpieces.

Toilets

Toilets in the low-to-moderate price range typically are two-piece units with a separate tank and bowl. More expensive models include one-piece types with integral tank and bowl and low-profile styles.

Standard toilets have 3.5-gallon tanks, but water-saver toilets, with 1.6-gallon tanks, are becoming increasingly common. Some municipalities and building codes even require water-saver toilets in new construction.

To install a two-piece toilet, anchor the bowl to the floor, then mount the tank onto the bowl. Toilets are made of vitreous china that cracks easily, so use care when handling them.

Toilets are typically installed after the floor covering is down. The horn in the toilet base fits into the toilet flange, which is solvent-glued to the drain pipe (inset). A wax ring and plastic sleeve prevent leaks at the base.

Installation Overview: Two-Piece Toilet

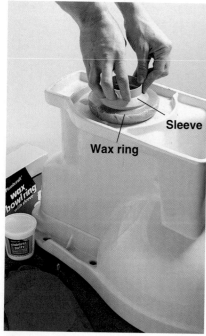

1 Turn the bowl upside down, and place a new wax ring and sleeve onto the toilet horn. Apply a ring of plumber's putty around the bottom edge of the toilet base.

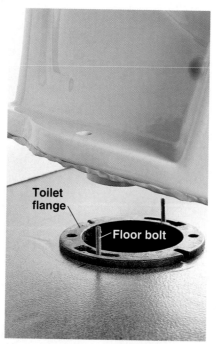

2 Set the bowl over the toilet flange so the bolts run through the holes in the base. Press down to compress the wax ring and putty. Secure the bowl with nuts.

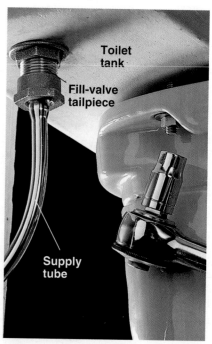

3 Attach the fill valve, handle, and flush valve assembly to the tank. Fit the tank on the bowl and secure it with the tank bolts. Connect the water supply to the fill valve.

82

Showers

The easiest way to build a shower is to use prefabricated shower stall panels and a plastic shower base. For a custom finish that takes a little more time, you can use ceramic tile.

Showers can be built in different sizes and configurations, but the basic elements are the same: There's a supply system, a drain system, and a framed alcove. The supply system consists of hot and cold water pipes leading to the faucet, which mixes the water and sends it up to the shower head. The drain system has a tailpiece and a P-trap that connects to the branch drain line. The alcove has 2 × 4 walls and a shower base set into a layer of mortar. Water-resistant wallboard provides adequate backing for prefab panels, but cementboard is a better backer for tile.

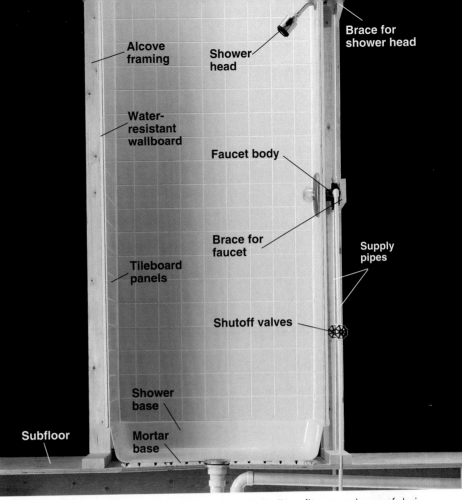

A basic shower stall has three framed walls built to fit around a prefabricated base. In an attic bathroom, the water supply pipes usually come from underneath the floor. In a basement, they enter from a side wall.

Installation Overview: Shower

1 Frame the alcove, centering it over the drain. Add braces for the supply pipes, faucet, and shower head. Cover the framing with water-resistant wallboard.

2 Pour a 1"-thick layer of dry-set mortar for the shower base. Set the shower base, fitting the drain tailpiece over drain pipe. Level the base, and let the mortar dry.

3 Prepare the shower stall panels by cutting holes for the faucet and shower head. Glue the panels to the walls, and support them with braces while the glue dries.

Wiring a Room

Your plans for wiring a room addition should reflect the ways you will use the space. For example, an attic sitting area should have a receptacle for an air conditioner, while a basement sewing room will need plenty of lighting. To determine your electrical needs, think about the finished space and the types of fixtures you plan to include. Also, consult the local building department to make sure your plans comply with local codes. The following are some of the basic electrical elements to consider.

The National Electrical Code requires receptacles to be spaced no more than 12 ft. apart, but for convenience you can space them as close as 6 ft. apart. You may need some non-standard receptacles, such as a GFCI (for bathrooms and wet areas), a 20-amp or 240-volt receptacle (for large appliances), and an isolated-ground receptacle (for a computer). Also consider the placement of furniture in the finished room; avoid placing receptacles or baseboard heaters where they may be blocked by furniture.

Lighting is an important consideration for every room, particularly rooms with limited sources of ambient light. Most codes require that each room have at

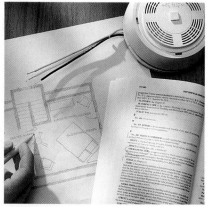

Draw plans that include all devices required by local codes.

Run extra wiring for computer, TV, speaker, and phone connections.

least one switch-controlled light fixture, with the switch placed near the room's entrance. Stairways must have lighting that illuminates each step, and the fixture must be controlled by three-way switches at the top and bottom landings. Hallways and closets also need switch-controlled lights. In addition to meeting code requirements, your lighting plan should include different types of lighting to provide versatility for everyday tasks, as well as visual warmth. This is especially true in basements, which generally need more artificial light than upper floors. It helps to use plenty of indirect lighting to eliminate shadows and provide ambient background light.

Your basement or attic rooms will also probably need additional wiring to supply auxiliary HVAC equipment. A typical bathroom vent fan or a ceiling fan runs on a standard 120-volt circuit, while most window air conditioners and baseboard heaters require 240-volt circuits. If you'll be installing an electric radiant heating system for supplemental heat, find out what type of circuit wiring the system requires.

One way to avoid long wiring runs and crowding of the main

Jeff Krueger©

Employ several different types of lighting to create an effective lighting scheme. Recessed, track, and under-cabinet light fixtures illuminate this basement with an attractive blend of lighting effects.

service panel is to install a circuit breaker subpanel in or near the finished space. A subpanel gets its power supply from a single cable leading from the main panel. With adequate amperage, a subpanel can serve all of the circuits necessary for the finished space—all from a convenient location.

Finally, don't forget the wiring that's not connected directly to the electrical panel, such as telephone lines and jacks, special cables for Internet access, speaker wiring, and coaxial cable for television and video connections. During a finishing project, it pays to run extra wiring for these types of connections. The minor expense of running additional wiring now will be more than offset by the convenience of having the wiring in place if you need it in the future. For coaxial cable and other communications wiring, be sure to maintain the recommended clearances from electrical cable, to avoid electrical interference.

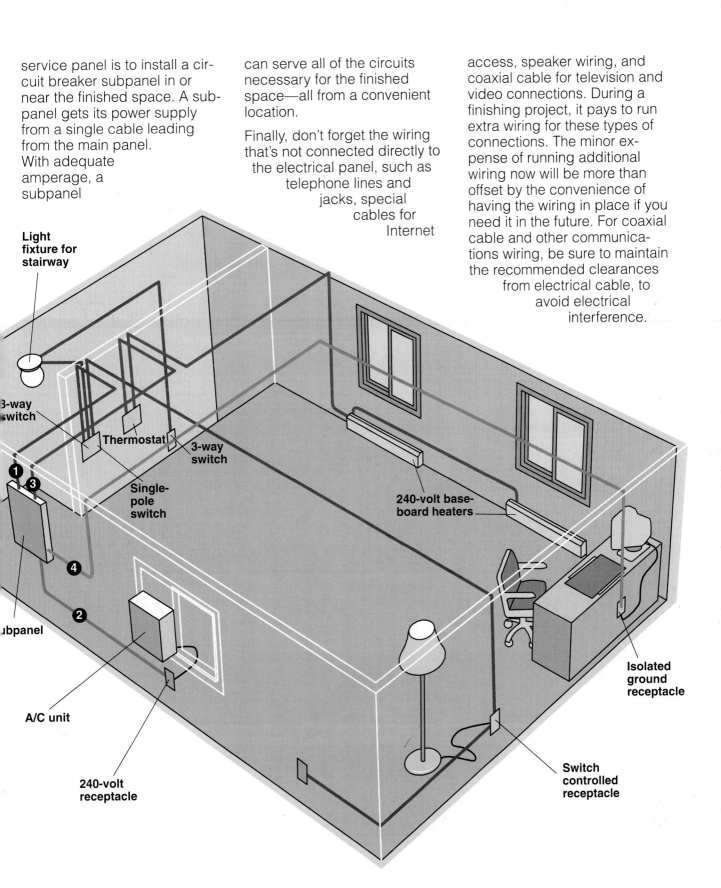

Map out electrical circuits for your room. The circuits for this attic room start at a subpanel, which is powered by the main service panel. *Circuit 1* controls the room's lighting and standard receptacles. *Circuit 2* feeds a 20-amp, 240-volt receptacle for a window air conditioner. *Circuit 3* is also a 240-volt circuit, providing power to a thermostat and two baseboard heater units. *Circuit 4* feeds an isolated ground receptacle for computer equipment. Circuits 2, 3, and 4 are dedicated circuits, meaning each serves only one device or series of heaters. See pages 86 to 87 for a closer look at these wiring layouts.

Wiring Diagrams

These diagrams show you the wiring configurations for the circuits found in the attic-room illustration on page 85. They include many of the common devices and wiring layouts for a basic wiring plan.

In these examples, the power sources for the circuits are supplied by a subpanel. The black wires in the diagrams are "hot," meaning they carry voltage; the white wires are "neutral," or zero-voltage, unless they are marked "coded for hot". The red wires in three-wire cables are used in different configurations to make hot, neutral, or ground connections. The green wires represent ground wires, each of which terminates at a grounding screw. In actual wiring, grounding wires are usually bare copper. Grounding screws are required in all metal electrical boxes, but plastic boxes do not need to be grounded.

The circuit cables represented in each configuration are standard non-metallic cable. The 240-volt circuits use 12-gauge cable; all other circuits are 15-amp and use 14-gauge cable.

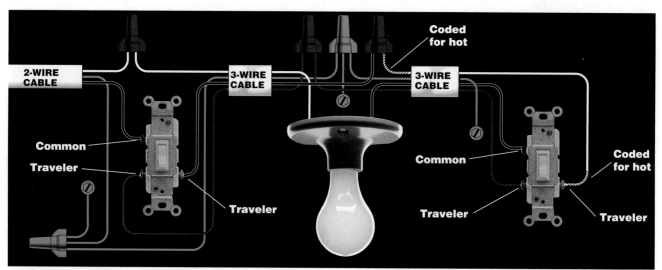

Three-way switches and light fixture: This configuration lets you control a light fixture from two locations. Each switch has one COMMON terminal and two TRAVELER terminals. Circuit wires attached to the TRAVELER screws run between the switches. Hot wires attached to the COMMON screws power the fixture.

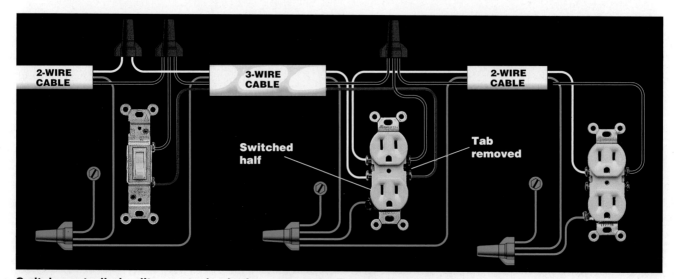

Switch-controlled split receptacle, duplex receptacle: This layout lets you use a switch to control a lamp plugged into a receptacle. Only the bottom half of the first receptacle is controlled by the switch; the remaining receptacle outlets are always hot. This configuration requires two-wire and three-wire cables.

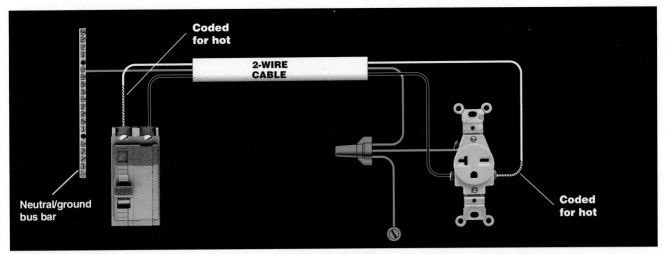

240-volt appliance receptacle: This layout includes a 20-amp, 240-volt dedicated appliance circuit that services a window air conditioner. The black and white circuit wires connected to a double-pole breaker each bring 120 volts of power to the receptacle. 12-gauge cable is used to accommodate the 20-amp current.

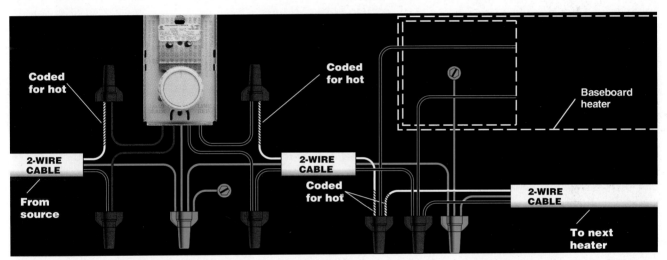

240-volt baseboard heaters: This configuration is typical for a series of 240-volt baseboard heaters controlled by a wall thermostat. All heaters in the circuit are wired as shown, except for the last heater, which is connected to only one cable. The circuit and cable sizes are determined by the total wattage of the heaters.

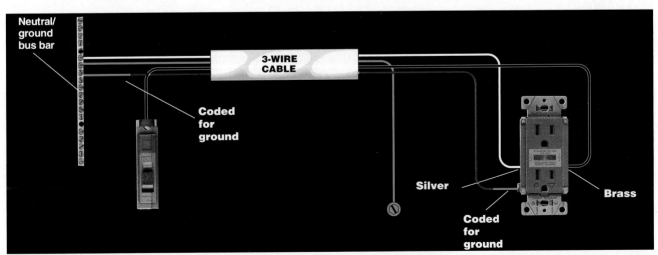

Dedicated 120-volt computer circuit, isolated ground receptacle: This circuit provides extra protection against power surges. The red wire in a 3-wire cable serves as an extra grounding conductor, connecting the grounding screw on an isolated ground receptacle directly to the grounding bus bar in the subpanel.

Incandescent Light Fixtures

Standard incandescent light fixtures are attached permanently to ceilings or walls. They include wall-hung sconces, ceiling-hung globe fixtures, and chandeliers. Most types are easy to install using basic tools.

Incandescent fixtures must mount to an electrical box that is attached either to the framing directly or by means of a metal brace that spans framing cavities. Wiring for most fixtures is simple. A two-wire circuit cable—with a black hot wire, a white neutral wire, and a ground wire—enters the box and is affixed by a cable clamp. The fixture itself has permanently attached wire *leads* for each light socket. To install the fixture, connect the wire leads to the circuit wires, using wire connectors, then mount the fixture to the box.

Incandescent light fixtures connect to the house circuit with pre-installed wire leads. Fixtures are secured directly to electrical boxes or to mounting straps attached to the boxes.

Labels in illustration: Circuit cable, Electrical box, Metal brace, Ground wires, Hot circuit wire, Neutral circuit wire, Hot leads, Neutral leads, Mounting strap, Socket, Fixture base, Shade

Installation Overview: Incandescent Light Fixture

1 Attach a fixture mounting strap to the electrical box, if the box does not already have one. The strap may have a preinstalled grounding screw.

Label: Grounding screw

2 Using wire connectors, connect the white wire lead to the white circuit wire, and the black lead to the black circuit wire. Attach the ground wire to the grounding screw on the mounting strap.

Labels: Ground wire, Wire leads

3 Attach the fixture base to the mounting strap, using the screws provided. Install a light bulb with a wattage rating consistent with the fixture rating, then attach the fixture globe.

Recessed Light Fixtures

Recessed light fixtures are especially popular for basement and attic finishing projects because they don't compromise valuable headroom.

You can mount recessed fixtures inside framed soffits or between ceiling joists, or you can attach them to a suspended ceiling grid. When attaching the fixtures to framing, install the fixtures and complete the wiring connections during the rough-in stage, before you install the wallboard or other ceiling material.

If your fixtures will be housed within an insulated ceiling, make sure they are rated *IC* (insulated ceiling), so that you can insulate up to and over the fixtures. Standard fixtures need 3" of clearance from any insulation. Always use IC fixtures in attic ceilings.

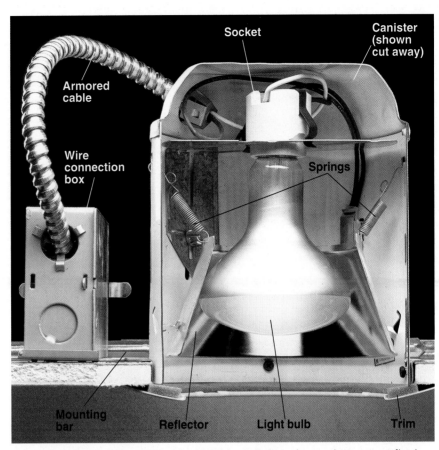

Recessed light fixtures are housed in metal canisters that mount flush with the ceiling finish material. Each fixture has its own wire connection box where the connections to the house circuit are made.

Installation Overview: Mounting a Recessed Light Fixture to Framing

1 Check the fixture's insulation rating. If the ceiling or soffit containing the fixtures will be insulated, make sure the fixtures are rated for insulated ceilings (IC).

2 Extend the fixture's mounting bars to reach the framing members, aligning the bars with the bottom faces of the framing. Drive the pointed ends of the bars into the framing.

3 Remove the wire connection box cover and open one knockout for each cable entering the box. Install a cable clamp for each open knockout.

89

Track lighting makes it easy to create custom lighting effects. The individual fixtures can be arranged to highlight art work, provide focused task lighting, or supply indirect lighting to brighten a dark corner.

Track Lighting

Track lighting is the most versatile type of permanent lighting. The tracks can be installed in any direction along walls and ceilings, and the fixtures can easily be moved anywhere along the track. A variety of styles of track lighting units are available in kits.

One advantage of track lighting is that an entire system can be powered by a single electrical box. The first track mounts over the box and is connected to the circuit wiring. Additional tracks are mounted to the ceiling and are tied into the first track with *L-connectors* or *T-connectors*. The lighting fixtures are individual units that connect to the tracks at any location.

Install the tracks and fixtures after the ceiling finish is in place. For the best effect, place tracks parallel to the wall closest to the fixture.

Installation Overview: Track Lighting

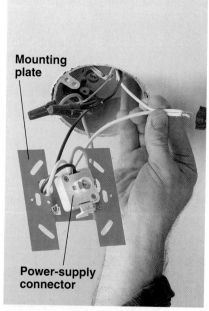

1 Connect the power-supply connector to the circuit wires, using wire connectors. Then, attach the mounting plate to the electrical box.

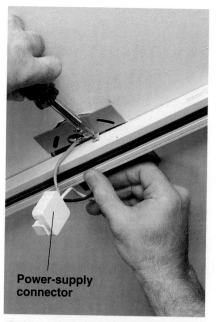

2 Mount the first track to the ceiling, screwing it into framing members or using toggle bolts. Secure the track to the mounting plate with screws. Snap the power-supply connector into the track.

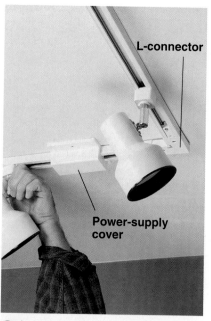

3 Install additional tracks, connecting them to the first track with L- or T-connectors. Install the power-supply cover. Cap bare track ends with dead-end pieces. Position the light fixtures as desired.

Baseboard Heaters

A baseboard heater is a simple electrical unit consisting of a heating element with attached metal fins for transferring heat and a *limit control*—a switch that prevents the element from overheating. To control temperature, some models have built-in thermostats; others are controlled by wall mounted thermostats that are wired directly to the heaters.

Typically a baseboard heater and its thermostat are hard-wired to a 240-volt circuit. In these circuits, both the black and white circuit wires are hot. Others types of heaters use only 120 volts. These may be hard-wired to a household circuit or plugged into a standard receptacle.

For best results, position baseboard heaters along outside walls, beneath windows.

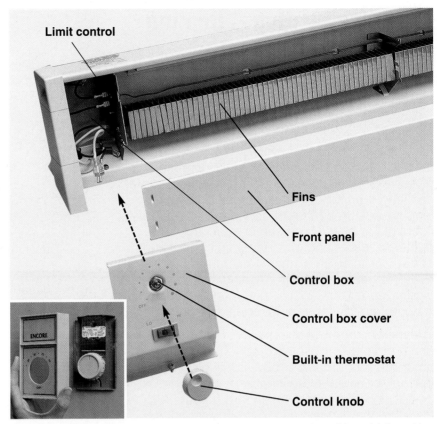

Limit control

Fins

Front panel

Control box

Control box cover

Built-in thermostat

Control knob

Baseboard heaters have control boxes that house the wiring. Units with control boxes at both ends usually can be wired at either end. Hard-wired heaters are often controlled by a wall-mounted thermostat (inset).

Installation Overview: Baseboard Heater (hard-wired)

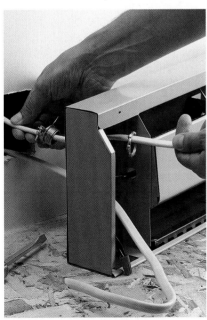

1 Feed the circuit cables into the connection box, and secure them with cable clamps. If there is more than one heater in the circuit, there will be two cables.

2 Position the heater against the wall, about 1" off the floor, and anchor it to the wall studs with screws. Strip away the cable sheathing so at least ¼" of sheathing extends into the connection box.

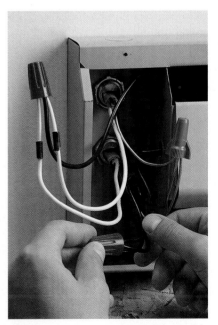

3 Make the wire connections with wire connectors, following the manufacturer's wiring diagram. For 240-volt circuits, tag the white wires with black tape to indicate they are hot. Install the box cover.

Providing Heating & Cooling

There are many options for supplying heat and air conditioning to your basement or attic. You can expand your home's central system, add a new system, or simply install some auxiliary heating or cooling appliances.

Expanding a forced-air system in a basement usually requires only a few added ducts (see pages 94-95). Running ducts to the attic is more challenging: often the easiest method is to extend a duct straight up through the intermediate floors of the house. You can conceal the new ducts in closets and other inconspicuous areas or frame and finish a small wall around them. A hydronic (water or steam) heating system can be expanded by adding new pipes and fixtures; this is a job for a plumber or mechanical contractor.

The main concern is whether your HVAC system can handle the additional load. If it cannot, and an upgraded furnace or boiler doesn't fit your budget, consider more localized supplemental units, such as electric baseboard heaters and room air conditioners. Both use normal household current and are controlled by their own thermostats, which provide better temperature control for specific rooms than a remote whole-house thermostat.

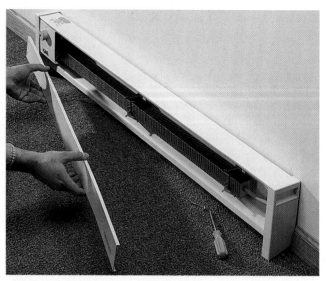

Electric baseboard heaters are a good option for rooms that need only supplemental or occasional heating. For best results, place them along exterior walls and under windows, and provide open space in front of the unit for air circulation.

Room A/C units typically plug into a 240-volt receptacle, while heaters either plug into a standard 120-volt receptacle or are hard-wired to a 240-volt circuit (see page 91). Either may require a new circuit in your electrical panel.

A gas fireplace is another good source of supplemental heat (see pages 150-156), and today's direct-vent fireplaces can be installed in almost any room. *Heater* models are designed to reach higher temperatures than standard models, and units with electric fans circulate warm air into the living space more efficiently.

Radiant heating systems are an increasingly popular option for remodels. These systems provide heat via electrical wires or hot-water tubing laid out in a ribbon pattern behind the finish surfaces of walls, ceilings, and floors. Radiant systems can supply dry, consistent heat to warm anything from a tiled floor in a half-bath to an entire basement slab. Large-scale radiant installations, however, are not for do-it-yourselfers.

In addition to mechanical systems, nature also plays a significant role in heating and cooling your home. Surrounded by earth, basements maintain a consistently cool temperature throughout the year, and in many climates need little or no air conditioning. Attics are just the opposite: they collect all the warm air that rises from the rooms below and can be difficult to cool. The natural ventilation provided by windows and skylights goes a long way to keeping attics comfortable during warm months.

Room air conditioners can be installed in windows or wall openings. Their cooling power is measured in Btus, and it's important to get a properly sized unit for the space it's cooling. For help with determining your cooling needs, contact the Association of Home Appliance Manufacturers (see page 157).

Radiant Heating Systems

Radiant heating systems come in many forms, but there are two general types: hydronic and electric. Hydronic systems use hot water—heated and circulated by a gas boiler—that flows through plastic or rubber tubing. One common installation method is to staple the tubing to the underside of the subfloor, which heats the floor above **(photo, top right)**. Another method is to set the tubing in a new slab of lightweight concrete. This can be a good option for heating basement floors if there's enough headroom to accommodate the new slab.

Electric systems are more versatile than hydronic systems and are great for providing heat to specific areas. For example, an electric mat system is designed to heat tiled floors. The heating mats can be installed directly over a concrete floor or over cementboard on wood floors. A layer of thin-set tile adhesive is troweled over the mat, and the tile is set into the adhesive **(photo, bottom right)**. The whole system is powered by a household circuit and controlled by a thermostat and timer.

Photo courtesy of Heatway Floor Heating & Snow Melting

Ventilating Attics

Windows and skylights provide effective, passive ventilation for attics. Opening the windows in the attic and the first floor of the house encourages natural circulation of cool air up through the floors. Whenever possible, install windows on opposing walls to create a cross-breeze when both windows are open. Room air conditioners also can help ventilate an attic by replacing stale indoor air with outdoor air. However, a single unit may not provide adequate ventilation for an entire attic. Check with the local building department for ventilation requirements in your area.

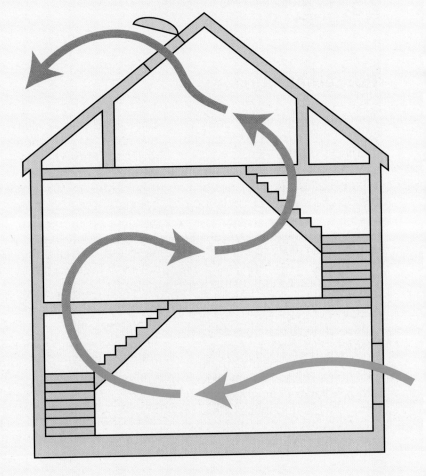

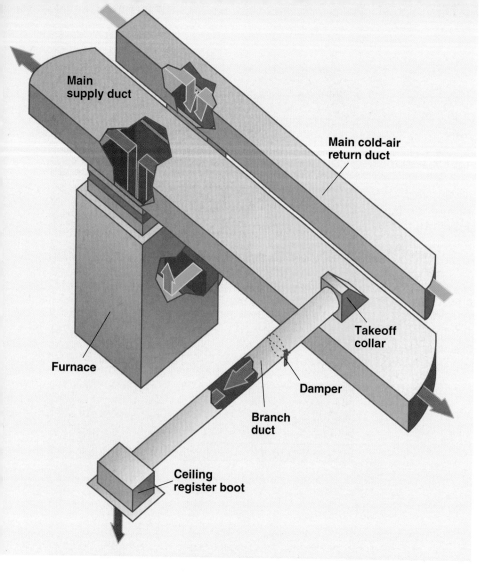

Main supply duct

Main cold-air return duct

Takeoff collar

Damper

Furnace

Branch duct

Ceiling register boot

Forced-Air Systems

A typical gas-furnace forced-air system has a main *supply* duct leading from the furnace and extending across the basement space just under the joists of the floor above. This duct supplies the warm air to the entire house via a network of *branch* ducts. The *return* ducts are just the reverse: They bring cool air from the rooms back to the furnace, providing air circulation throughout the house. (To find out which is which, turn on the furnace and feel the ducts: Supply ducts will be warm, return ducts cool.) The whole system is balanced by adjustable *dampers* located inside the branch ducts and controlled by the home's thermostat.

Some systems—called *zone systems*—are balanced by several automatic dampers. Each damper is controlled by its own thermostat, thus maintaining a consistent temperature within a specific zone. Zone systems are complicated, and you'll need the help of an HVAC specialist to expand the system.

With standard systems, providing heat and air conditioning to remodeled spaces is fairly straightforward. While you're planning the walls and thinking about which rooms are going where, have an HVAC specialist take a look at your system. He or she can help you find the best way to distribute air to the new space without compromis-

ing service to the rest of the house.

In most cases, you can run new branch ducts directly from the main supply duct or from another branch duct and use empty wall-stud cavities to serve as branch cold-air return ducts. Page 95 shows you the major steps of installing a new branch supply duct in a basement space. Here are a few tips to help you with the planning:

• Plan branch ducts with as few turns as possible; air moves most efficiently through short, straight runs of duct.

• Round, galvanized metal duct is the most efficient for moving air, while flexible duct is about the least. Use flexible duct only where metal isn't practical. To save space, you may be able to use shallow rectangular metal duct that fits between studs and joists.

• Locate supply registers near exterior walls, below or above windows, if possible. Include at least one in each room. Place return air inlets on walls opposite the supply registers, to draw heated or cooled air across the space. To avoid circulating moist and odorous air through the system, do not place cold-air return inlets in bathrooms or kitchens.

• To get an idea of the size of branch ducts you'll need, examine the existing ductwork. Note the sizes and lengths of the branch ducts and the dimensions of the rooms they serve, then compare those with the new space.

• If possible, run ducts inside clear joist cavities. Where ducts must run beneath joists, route them through closets (or behind kneewalls in attics), to minimize the number of soffits necessary to conceal them.

Installation Overview: Branch Supply Duct

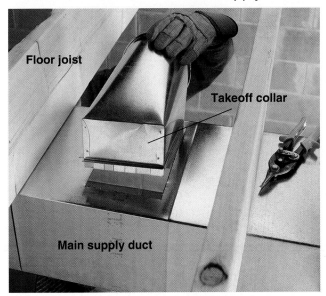

Floor joist

Takeoff collar

Main supply duct

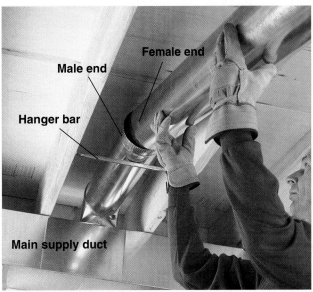

Male end

Female end

Hanger bar

Main supply duct

1 Attach a starting collar to the main duct. A *takeoff* collar mounts to the top or side of the main duct; a *straight* collar mounts to the side. Cut a hole into the duct to accept the tabbed end of the collar, using aviation snips. Fit the collar in the hole, then secure it by bending over the tabs inside the duct. Secure two of the tabs with self-tapping sheet metal screws.

2 Run the branch duct out to the register boot location (see step 3). Starting from the main duct, install full sections of duct by fitting their plain female ends over their crimped male ends. The crimped ends should point away from the main duct. Use hanger bars or straps to support the sections temporarily as you work. Fasten the sections together with two sheet metal screws.

How to Build a Cold-air Return Duct

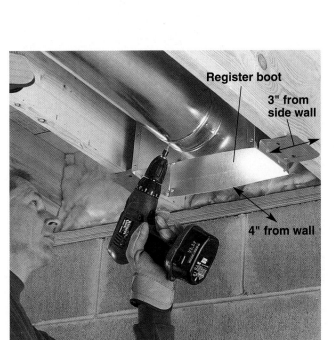

Register boot

3" from side wall

4" from wall

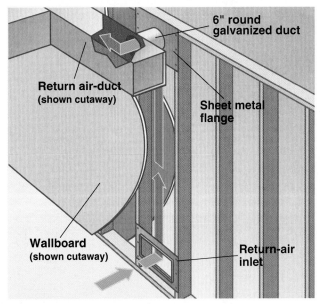

6" round galvanized duct

Return air-duct (shown cutaway)

Sheet metal flange

Wallboard (shown cutaway)

Return-air inlet

3 Install the register boot, then attach the final duct section. Position the boot so that the long side is at least 4" from the room's long wall and the short side is at least 3" from any side wall. Mount the boot to the joists. If you need to shorten the final section of duct, cut from the plain end, and use a connecting band, if necessary, to join the last two duct sections. Attach the final section to the boot with screws. Install permanent hanger bars or straps every 4 to 6 ft. along the duct.

Cold-air return ducts often consist of enclosed stud or joist cavities with an air inlet at one end and a boot or fitting at the other end that feeds into a branch duct. The cavities may be enclosed with wallboard or subflooring, or with flat metal sheeting nailed to the framing members. To ensure adequate air flow, the cavity should not hold plumbing or blocking, but a few wires are usually acceptable.

Photo courtesy of Armstrong Ceilings

Finishing Walls & Ceilings

At this stage in the remodeling project, much of the heavy work is done. You've completed the framing and rough-ins, and now it's time to install insulation and cover everything up with finish materials. It's a satisfying process to transform the skeletal maze of framing into cleanly defined rooms, and your success with this step will not only affect the look of your finished rooms but will also help determine how comfortable they will be throughout the seasons.

Insulating is an easy, if unpleasant, chore that most people do themselves, but it's important to complete this job properly. You'll need to find out what insulating techniques work best in your area. For example, houses in some climates must have vapor barriers installed over the insulation to keep moisture from rotting the framing. And roof insulation is especially important in cold regions, where finishing an attic can create problems if the roof is not effectively insulated and ventilated. You may also want to insulate your floors, ceilings, and interior walls for soundproofing.

After the insulation comes the fun job of deciding what materials you'll use to finish the walls and ceilings. Wallboard is the most common finish used by do-it-yourself remodelers. It's inexpensive and easy to install, and it provides a smooth, flat surface for paint or wallcoverings. Tongue-and-groove paneling is a bit more challenging to install, but the result is a warm, natural-wood finish that you can't get with wallboard. The paneling project in this section shows you a basic installation procedure that you can apply to different paneling treatments. A popular choice for basement projects is a suspended ceiling, which is particularly suitable for an informal room. A suspended ceiling makes it easy to cover the many service lines running through a basement, and it provides quick access to shutoff valves and drain cleanouts.

But before you cover your walls and ceiling with any material, make sure you have the approval from the building inspector on everything that lies within them; you won't want to tear down your newly finished wallboard because the inspector didn't check your wiring staples.

Installing Fiberglass Insulation

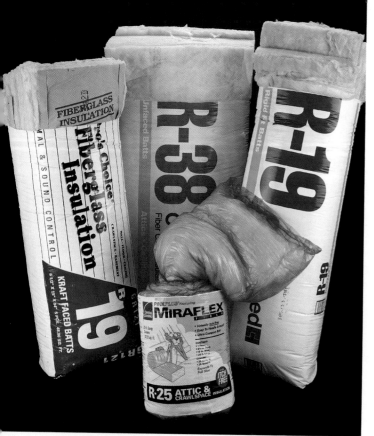

Fiberglass insulation comes in *batts* cut to length for standard stud-wall bays as well as long rolls. Various options include: kraft-paper and foil facings, which serve as vapor barriers (some foils are flame-resistant); plastic-encapsulated blankets; high density blankets (for rafters); and standard, unfaced rolls and batts. Standard widths fit between 16- and 24"-on-center framing.

Handling fiberglass is a lot less uncomfortable when you're dressed for it. Wear pants and a long-sleeve shirt, gloves, goggles, and a good-quality dust mask or respirator. Shower as soon as you finish the installation.

Before you insulate your basement or attic (or even buy insulation), ask the local building department about two things: *R-value* and *vapor barriers*. All insulation has an R-value clearly printed on its packaging. This is the measure of how well the insulation keeps in the heat and keeps out the cold, and vice versa. The higher the R-value, the better the insulation works—and the thicker it is. The building department will tell you what R-values you need for your walls and ceilings, and whether the insulation job must be inspected before you cover it.

Vapor barriers come in a few different forms, but all have a common purpose. They prevent the water vapor present in warm indoor air from passing beyond the wall or ceiling surface and through the framing, where it contacts cold exterior surfaces and condenses. This condensation promotes mildew growth that can rot the framing and insulation. Vapor barriers are required in most seasonal climates and are typically installed on the "warm-in-winter" side of exterior walls and attic ceilings, between the insulation and the interior finish material.

Paper- and foil-faced and encapsulated insulation have their own vapor barriers, but for a more effective, continuous barrier, use a layer of 6-mil polyethylene sheeting stapled to framing members over unfaced insulation. Also be aware that faced insulation comes with a few drawbacks. The paper tears easily, and facings make it difficult to cut around obstacles. And, if you trim a batt to fit into a narrow bay, you lose the facing flange—and thus the vapor seal—on one side. Also, most facings are flammable and must be covered with wallboard or other approved finish, even in unfinished areas, such as storage rooms. One alternative is to use insulation with an approved flame-resistant foil facing.

The most important part of insulating is making sure there are no gaps between the insulation and framing, around obstructions, or between insulation pieces. The idea is to create a continuous "thermal envelope" that keeps interior air from contacting outdoor temperatures.

Everything You Need:

Tools: Utility knife, stapler.

Materials: Fiberglass insulation, 6-mil polyethylene sheeting, staples, packing tape.

Tips for Installing Fiberglass Insulation

Never compress insulation to fit into a narrow space. Instead, use a sharp utility knife to trim the blanket about ¼" wider and longer than the space. To trim, hold the blanket in place and use a wall stud as a straightedge and cutting surface.

Insulate around pipes, wires, and electrical boxes by peeling the blanket in half and sliding the back half behind the obstruction. Then, lay the front half in front of the obstruction. Cut the front half to fit snugly around boxes.

Use scraps of insulation to fill gaps around window and door jambs. Fill the cavities loosely to avoid compressing the insulation. Fill narrow gaps with expanding spray-foam insulation, following manufacturer's instructions.

How to Install Vapor Barriers

Facing flange

Provide a vapor barrier using faced insulation by tucking along the edges of the insulation until the facing flange is flush with the edge of the framing. Make sure the flanges lie flat, with no wrinkles or gaps, and staple them to the faces of the framing members about every 8". Patch any gaps or facing tears with packing tape or a construction tape supplied by the manufacturer.

Install a polyethylene vapor barrier by draping the sheeting over the entire wall or ceiling, extending it a few inches beyond the perimeter. Staple the sheeting to the framing, and overlap sheets at least 12". Carefully cut around obstructions. Seal around electrical boxes and other penetrations with packing tape. Trim excess sheeting along the ceiling and floor after you install the finish material.

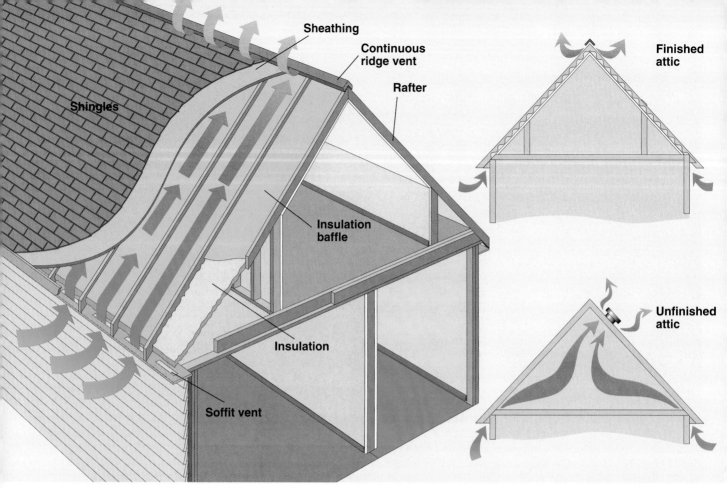

A roof ventilation system works in conjunction with attic insulation: Insulation forms a thermal barrier that keeps in the home's conditioned air, while the ventilation system uses outdoor air to keep the roof deck cool and dry. In most unfinished attics, the entire attic space is ventilated, and proper air flow can be achieved with roof vents or gable-wall vents.

Insulating & Ventilating Roofs

Ventilation works in concert with insulation to keep your roof deck healthy. Roofs need ventilation for a number of reasons. During hot weather, direct sunlight can heat a roof considerably, and air flow underneath the roof deck helps lower temperatures, keeping your attic cooler. In cold climates, and particularly in areas with heavy snowfall, roofs need ventilation to prevent ice dams and other moisture problems. As you insulate your attic ceiling, you need to make sure the roof will remain properly ventilated.

Here's how roof ventilation works: Air intake vents installed in the soffits—called *soffit vents*—allow outdoor air to pass under the roof sheathing and flow up toward the ridge, where it exits through one or more exhaust vents. In unfinished attics, with insulation only along the floor, air is allowed to flow from open rafter bays into a common air space under the roof. It can then be exhausted through any of the roof or gable vents. When you finish your attic, however, you enclose

part or all of each rafter bay with insulation and a ceiling finish. A flat attic ceiling will provide some open air space above the ceiling, but air flow still may be limited. With a peaked ceiling, the rafter bays are enclosed up to the ridge, and a single roof vent can serve only one rafter bay. To improve ventilation, you can install additional roof and soffit vents or a continuous ridge vent, which provides ventilation to all of the rafter bays.

A roof ventilation system must have a clear air path between the intake and exhaust vents. For this reason, most building codes call for 1" of air space between the insulation and the roof sheathing. To ensure this air space remains unobstructed, install insulation baffles in the rafter bays. Also be sure to install enough insulation to meet the recommended R-value for your area. This may require increasing the depth of your attic rafters to accommodate the insulation and baffles. For more information on insulation R-values and installation, see pages 98-99.

Tips for Insulating Roofs

Increase the rafter depth to make room for thicker insulation by attaching 2 × 2s to the rafter edges. Fasten the 2 × 2s with 3"-long, countersunk screws. You can also save space by using high-density insulation.

Use insulation baffles to provide a continuous air channel behind the insulation. The baffles should start just in front of the exterior walls' top plates and extend up to the vents. Attach the baffles to the roof sheathing with staples.

Lay fiberglass insulation, stopping short of the baffle opening to avoid restricting air flow. Insulation in the attic floor should cover the exterior walls' top plates but not extend into the soffit cavities.

Options for Ventilating Roofs

Photo courtesy of Airvent Inc.

Roof vents (box- or mushroom-type) are commonly used to ventilate unfinished attics. You can improve ventilation by adding more roof vents and soffit vents (inset). If your rafter bays are enclosed all the way to the ridge, be sure the soffit vents and roof vents are installed along the same rafter bays.

Continuous ridge vents are the most effective roof vents, because they ventilate along the entire ridge. It costs less to have one installed during a re-roofing project, but they can be installed onto an existing roof that's in good condition. This type of vent works best when used in conjunction with continuous soffit vents (inset).

New wallboard

2 × 4 framing

Old wallboard

Sound-board

Add soundproofing materials before and after the walls and ceilings are covered. If the framing is exposed, add fiberglass insulation to reduce sound travel between rooms. To soundproof an existing wall that's finished, add layers of wallboard, acoustical tile, or soundboard—a fiber panel product that absorbs sound.

Soundproofing Walls & Ceilings

One of the more common reasons people finish their attics or basements is to create spaces for getting away from everyday household activity and noise. Perhaps you're planning a quiet reading space, a home office, or a home theater. All of these rooms will be more enjoyable to use if their walls and ceilings are properly soundproofed.

Wall and ceiling construction is rated for sound transmission by a system called Sound Transmission Class (STC). The higher the STC rating, the quieter the house. For example, if a wall is rated at 30 to 35 STC, loud speech can be understood through the wall. At 42 STC, loud speech is reduced to a murmur. At 50 STC, loud speech cannot be heard. Standard construction methods typically result in a 32 STC rating, while soundproofed walls and ceilings can carry a rating of up to 48 STC.

Basic soundproofing materials include fiberglass insulation, acoustical tile, soundboard, ⅝" wallboard, and resilient steel channels or *sound channels*. Sound channels are used to anchor wallboard to walls and ceilings, and they reduce sound transmission by absorbing vibrations. Page 103 shows you some applications of different soundproofing materials and their STC ratings.

In addition to using soundproofing materials in your walls and ceilings, it's important to seal any air leaks between rooms. Sound travels through air, and even small air passages between rooms can destroy your efforts at soundproofing. Block air by caulking around electrical boxes and other penetrations after the finish materials are in place. Also seal along the bottoms and tops of walls and around door jambs. Install door sweeps to stop air underneath doors.

Tips for Soundproofing Existing Floors & Ceilings

Reduce sound through basement ceilings by adding carpeting and padding on the floor above and installing fiberglass insulation in the joist cavities. Install ⅝" wallboard on the basement ceiling, attached to sound channels. The rating for this system is 48 STC.

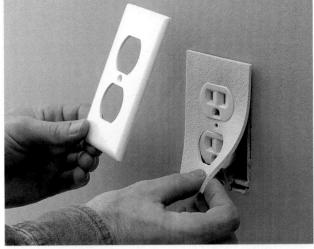

Seal air passages between walls with caulk, expanding foam, and neoprene slips. Use caulk or foam to seal along the bottoms of walls and around door frames. Install neoprene slips behind the coverplates of electrical boxes.

Soundproofing Walls & Ceilings (walls shown cut away)	Sound Transmission Class
Typical utility area stud wall, unfinished on one side.	28 STC
Spaces between framing members filled with fiberglass insulation (A) and stud wall covered with wallboard.	39 STC
Extra layer of wallboard attached to wall, using sound channels (B).	44 STC
Acoustical tile (C) attached to an insulated stud wall, using construction adhesive or staples.	46 STC

Installing & Finishing Wallboard

Wallboard is commonly available in 4 × 8-ft. and 4 × 12-ft. panels, in thicknesses ranging from ¼" to ¾". The panels are tapered along their long edges so that adjoining panels form a slightly recessed seam that you finish with paper tape and wallboard compound. End-to-end joints are more difficult to finish, so avoid end-butted seams whenever possible. And to minimize the number of joints that need finishing, use the longest panels you can safely handle; just make sure you can get them into the workspace.

Use ½"- or ⅝"-thick panels on ceilings. Thinner panels are lighter and easier to work with, but ⅝" wallboard provides better sound insulation and is less likely to sag over time. Use ½" panels on walls. Install wallboard on the ceiling first, then finish the walls, butting the wall panels snug against the ceiling panels to give them extra support.

Everything You Need:

Tools: Wallboard T-square, utility knife, jig saw, wallboard compass, chalk line, rented wallboard lift, drill or screwgun, lifter, 4-ft. level, 4", 6", 10" and 12" wallboard knives, pole sander.

Materials: Wallboard, 1¼" wallboard screws, compound, joint tape, corner bead, sandpaper.

Tips for Preparing Walls & Ceilings for Wallboard

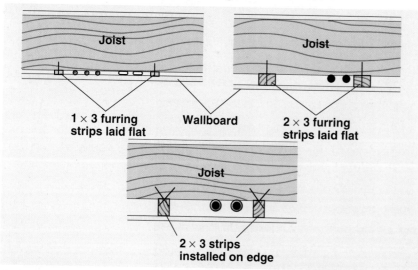

Joist

1 × 3 furring strips laid flat   Wallboard

Joist

2 × 3 furring strips laid flat

Joist

2 × 3 strips installed on edge

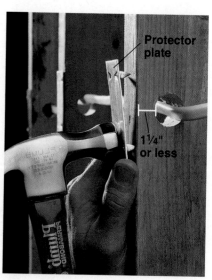

Protector plate

1¼" or less

Attach furring strips to framing where service lines and other obstacles project beyond the framing. The strips create a flat surface for attaching wallboard. Use 1 × 3 or 2 × 3 furring strips and attach them perpendicular to the framing, using wallboard screws. Space the strips 16" or 24" on center so that they provide support for all of the wallboard edges.

Use protector plates where wires or pipes pass through framing members and are less than 1¼" from the front edge. The plates prevent wallboard screws from puncturing wires or pipes.

How to Cut Wallboard

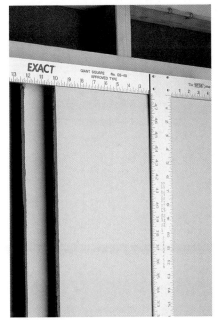

1 To make vertical cuts, set the wallboard panel against a wall with the front side facing out. Mark the desired length on the face, then position a wallboard T-square at the mark. Hold the square in place with your hand and foot, and cut through the face paper, using a utility knife.

Tip: Make horizontal cuts by extending a tape measure to the desired width of the cut, and hooking a utility knife blade under the end of the tape. Grip the tape tightly in one hand and the utility knife in the other, and move both hands along the panel to cut through the face paper.

2 Bend the scored section backwards with both hands to break the gypsum core of the wallboard. Fold back the unwanted piece, and cut through the back paper with the utility knife.

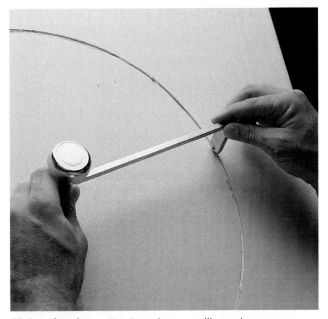

Make square internal cuts, such as openings for electrical boxes, using a jig saw fitted with a coarse wood-cutting blade or a wallboard keyhole saw. To start the cut, set the base of the saw on the panel and pivot the saw downward until the blade cuts through the panel, then finish the cut with the base flat against the panel.

Make circular cutouts using a wallboard compass. Mark the centerpoint of the cutout, then set the point of the compass on the mark. Press down and rotate the compass to score through the paper. Tap a nail through the centerpoint to mark the other side. Score the back-side paper, then knock out the hole through front side with a hammer.

How to Install Wallboard on a Ceiling

1 Create a control line by measuring out from the top plate of the adjoining wall. Make a mark on the outermost joists (or rafters) at 48⅛", then snap a chalk line through the marks. The line should be perpendicular to the joists. Use the control line to align the first row of panels and to measure for cutouts.

2 Measure across the joists to make sure the first panel will break on the center of a joist. If necessary, cut the panel from the end that abuts the side wall so that the panel breaks on the next farthest joist. Load the panel onto a rented wallboard lift, and hoist the panel until it rests flat against the joists.

3 Position the panel so the side edge is even with the control line and the leading end is centered on a joist. Fasten the panel using 1¼" wallboard screws. Drive a screw every 8" along the edges and every 12" in the field (consult the local building department for fastening requirements in your area).

4 After the first row of panels is installed, begin the next row with a half-panel of wallboard. This ensures that the butted end joints will be staggered between rows.

How to Install Wallboard on Walls

1 Plan the wallboard placement so there are no joints at the corners of doors or windows. Wallboard joints at corners often crack or cause bulges that interfere with window and door trim.

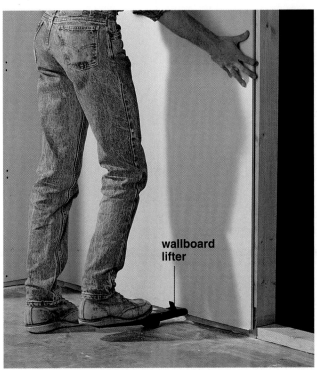

2 Install wallboard panels vertically unless the panels are long enough to span the wall sideways. Lift the panels tight against the ceiling with wallboard lifter. Plumb the first panel with a 4-ft. level, making sure the panel breaks on the center of a stud.

wallboard lifter

3 Anchor the panels to the framing with 1¼" wallboard screws. Drive a screw every 8" along the edges and every 12" in the field of the panel. Drive the screws so their heads are just below the surfaces of the panels, creating a slight depression in the face paper without breaking through it.

Tip: Unsupported wallboard edges tend to crack and sag, ruining your finishing work. When installing new wallboard next to an existing wall surface, or where the framing layout does not coincide with the wallboard edges, you may need to add 1 × or 2 × lumber backing to support wallboard edges.

How to Tape Wallboard Joints

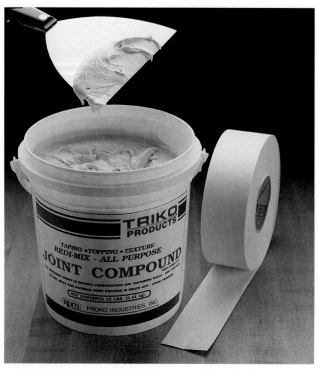

Tip: Use premixed wallboard compound for most taping and finishing jobs to eliminate messy mixing and lumpy results. When using premixed compound, also use paper wallboard joint tape.

1 Apply a thin layer of wallboard compound over the joint with a 4" or 6" wallboard knife. Load the knife by dipping it into a wallboard mud pan filled with wallboard compound.

2 Press the wallboard tape into the compound immediately, centering the tape over the joint. Smooth over the tape firmly with the 6" knife to flatten the tape and squeeze out excess compound from behind it. Let the compound dry completely.

3 Apply two thin finish coats of compound with a 10" or 12" wallboard knife. Allow the second coat to dry and shrink overnight before applying the final coat. Let the final coat dry completely before sanding.

How to Finish Inside Corners

1 Fold a strip of paper wallboard tape in half by pinching the strip and pulling it between your thumb and forefinger.

2 Apply a thin layer of wallboard compound to both sides of the inside corner, using a 4" or 6" wallboard knife. Position the end of the folded tape strip at the top of the joint and press the tape into the wet compound with the knife. Smooth both sides of the corner to flatten the tape and remove excess compound. Apply two finish coats of compound.

How to Finish Outside Corners

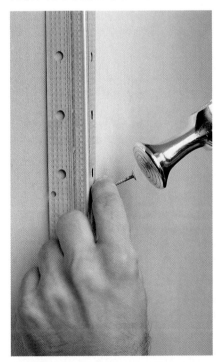

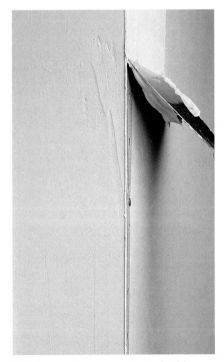

1 Position metal corner bead on the outside corners, making sure the bead is centered along the corner. Attach the bead with 1¼" wallboard nails or screws spaced 8" apart.

2 Cover the corner bead with three coats of wallboard compound, using a 6" or 10" wallboard knife. Let each coat dry and shrink overnight before applying the next coat. Sand the final coat smooth.

Tip: Sand the finished joints lightly after the wallboard compound dries, using a pole sander and wallboard sandpaper or a sanding sponge. Wear a dust mask and goggles when sanding.

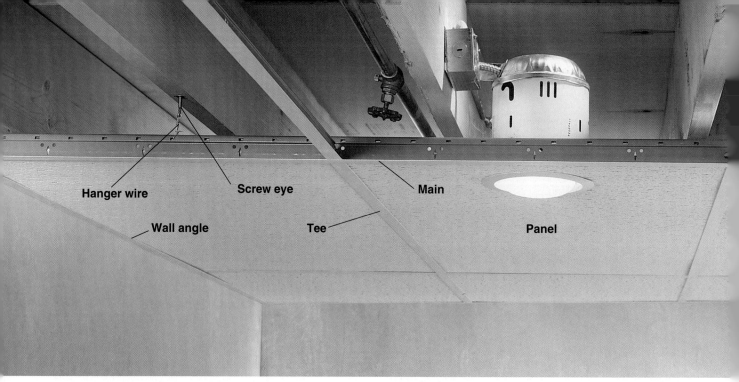

Hanger wire   **Screw eye**   **Main**

Wall angle   **Tee**   **Panel**

Suspended ceilings are great for basements because they provide access to mechanicals and are easy to install over uneven joists. You can also install recessed or fluorescent light fixtures that mount flush to the ceiling surface.

Installing a Suspended Ceiling

Suspended ceilings have some advantages over standard ceiling finishes (such as wallboard). Because all of the panels can be removed, virtually everything behind a suspended ceiling, like plumbing runs, shut-off valves, and wiring, is easily accessible. Also, suspended ceilings can compensate for uneven joists.

One notable disadvantage of suspended ceilings is that they take up headroom. Typically, suspended ceilings should hang about 4" below the lowest obstacle, to leave enough room for installing or removing the panels. So, before you decide on using a suspended system, measure to determine the finished ceiling height and make sure it will comply with the local building code.

A suspended ceiling is a grid framework made of lightweight metal brackets hung on wires attached to ceiling or floor joists. The frame consists of T-shaped main beams (mains) and cross-tees (tees), and L-shaped wall angles. The grid supports ceiling panels that rest on the flanges of the framing pieces. Ceiling panels come in 2 × 2-ft. or 2 × 4-ft. sections. They're available in a variety of styles, including insulated panels, acoustical tiles that dampen sound, and light-diffuser panels that are used with fluorescent light fixtures. Generally, metal-frame ceiling systems are more durable than ones made of plastic.

To begin your ceiling project, determine the panel layout based on the width and length of the room. Often, some panels must be cut to accommodate the room. Place trimmed panels on opposite sides of your ceiling for a balanced look, as when installing floor tile or ceramic wall tile. You'll also want to install your ceiling so it's perfectly level. An inexpensive but effective tool for marking a level line around a room perimeter is a water level. You can make a water level by purchasing two water-level ends (available at hardware stores and home centers) and attaching them to a standard garden hose.

Although suspended ceilings work well for hiding mechanicals in a basement, it looks best if you build soffits around low obstructions, such as support beams and large ducts (see pages 57-59). Finish the soffits with wallboard, and install the ceiling wall angle to the soffit.

Everything You Need:

Tools: Water level, chalk line, drill, screw-eye driver, aviation snips, dryline, lock-type clamps, pliers, straightedge, utility knife.

Materials: Suspended ceiling kit (frame), screw eyes, hanger wires, ceiling panels, 1½" wallboard screws or masonry nails.

Tips for Installing a Suspended Ceiling

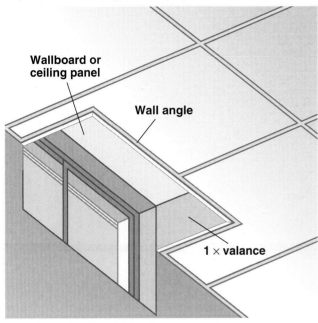

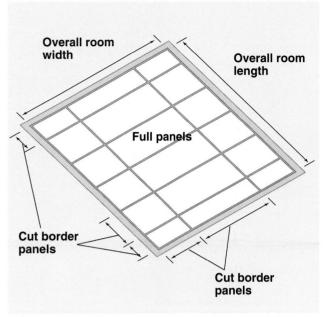

Build a valance around basement awning windows so they can be opened fully. Attach 1 × lumber of an appropriate width to joists or blocking. Install wallboard (or a suspended-ceiling panel trimmed to fit) to the joists inside the valance.

Draw your ceiling layout on paper, based on the exact dimensions of the room. Plan so that trimmed border panels on opposite sides of the room are of equal width and length (avoid panels smaller than ½-size). If you include lighting fixtures in your plan; make sure they follow the grid layout.

How to Install a Suspended Ceiling

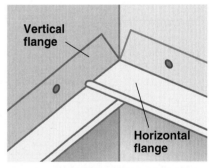

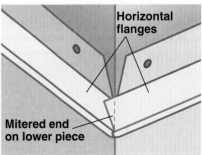

1 Make a mark on one wall that indicates the ceiling height plus the height of the wall angle. Use a water level to transfer that height to both ends of each wall. Snap a chalk line to connect the marks. This line indicates the top of the ceiling's wall angle.

2 Attach wall angle pieces to the studs on all walls, positioning the top of the wall angle flush with the chalk line. Use 1½" wallboard screws (or short masonry nails driven into mortar joints on concrete block walls). Cut angle pieces using aviation snips.

Tip: Trim wall angle pieces to fit around corners. At inside corners (top), back-cut the vertical flanges slightly, then overlap the horizontal flanges. At outside corners (bottom), miter-cut one horizontal flange, and overlap the flanges.

(continued next page)

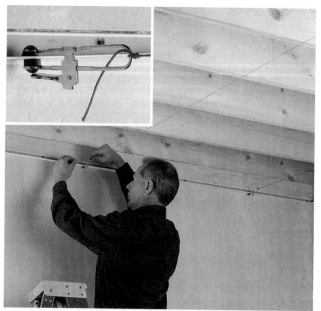

3 Mark the location of each main on the wall angles at the ends of the room. The mains must be parallel to each other and perpendicular to the ceiling joists. Set up a guide string for each main, using a thin dryline and lock-type clamps (inset). Clamp the strings to the opposing wall angles, stretching them very taut so there's no sagging.

4 Install screw eyes for hanging the mains, using a drill and screw-eye driver. Drill pilot holes and drive the eyes into the joists every 4 ft., locating them directly above the guide strings. Attach hanger wire to the screw eyes by threading one end through the eye and twisting the wire on itself at least three times. Trim excess wire, leaving a few inches of wire hanging below the level of the guide string.

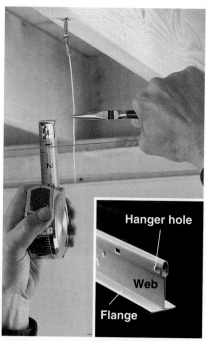

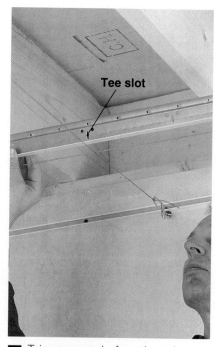

5 Measure the distance from the bottom of a main's flange to the hanger hole in the web (inset). Use this measurement to prebend each hanger wire. Measure up from the guide string and make a 90° bend in the wire, using pliers.

6 Following your ceiling plan, mark the placement of the first tee on opposite wall angles at one end of the room. Set up a guide string for the tee, using a dryline and clamps, as before. This string must be perpendicular to the guide strings for the mains.

7 Trim one end of each main so that a tee slot in the main's web is aligned with the tee guide string, and the end of the main bears fully on a wall angle. Set the main in place to check the alignment of the tee slot with the string.

8 Cut the other end of each main to fit, so that it rests on the opposing wall angle. If a single main cannot span the room, splice two mains together, end-to-end (the ends should be fashioned with male-female connectors). Make sure the tee slots remain aligned when splicing.

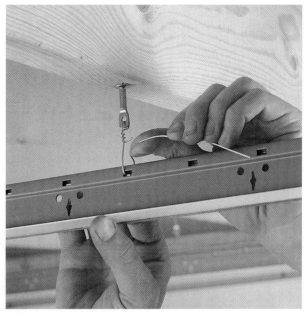

9 Install the mains by setting the ends on the wall angle and threading the hanger wires through the hanger holes in the webs. The wires should be as close to vertical as possible. Wrap each wire around itself three times, making sure the main's flange is level with the main guide string. Also install a hanger near each main splice.

10 Attach tees to the mains, slipping their tabbed ends into the tee slots on the mains. Align the first row of tees with the tee guide string; install the remaining rows at 4-ft. intervals. If you're using 2 × 2-ft. panels, install 2-ft. cross-tees between the midpoints of the 4-ft. tees. Cut and install the border tees, setting the tee ends on the wall angles. Remove all guide strings and clamps.

11 Place full ceiling panels into the grid first, then install the border panels. Lift the panels in at an angle, and position them so they rest on the frame's flanges. Reach through adjacent openings to adjust the panels, if necessary. To trim the border panels to size, cut them face-up, using a straightedge and a utility knife (inset).

Paneling an Attic Ceiling

Tongue-and-groove paneling offers a warm, attractive finish that's especially suited to the angles of an attic ceiling. Pine is the most common material for tongue-and-groove paneling, but you can choose from many different wood species and panel styles. Panels are typically ⅜" to ¾" thick and are often attached directly to ceiling joists and rafters. Some building codes require the installation of wallboard as a fire stop behind ceiling paneling that's thinner than ¼".

When purchasing your paneling, get enough material to cover about 15% more square footage than the actual ceiling size to allow for waste. Since the tongue portions of panels slip into the grooves of adjacent pieces, square footage for paneling is based on the *reveal*. The reveal is the exposed face of the panels after they are installed (see step 1, page 115).

Tongue-and-groove boards can be attached with flooring nails or finish nails. Flooring nails hold better because they have spiraled shanks, but they tend to have larger heads than finish nails. Whenever possible, drive the nails through the base of the tongue and into the framing. This is called *blind-nailing,* because the groove of the succeeding board covers the nail heads. Add face-nails only at joints and in locations where more support is needed, such as along the first and last boards. And to ensure clean cuts, use a compound miter saw. These saws are especially useful for ceilings with non-90° angles.

Layout is crucial to the success of a paneling project. Before you start, measure and calculate to see how many boards will be installed, using the reveal measurement. If the final board will be less than 2" wide, trim the first, or *starter*, board by cutting the long edge that abuts the wall. If the ceiling peak is not parallel to the side (starting) wall, you must compensate for the difference by ripping the starter piece at an angle. The leading edge of the starter piece, and every piece thereafter, must be parallel to the peak.

Everything You Need:

Tools: Chalk line, compound miter saw, circular saw, drill, nail set.

Materials: Tongue-and-groove paneling, 1¾" spiral flooring nails, trim molding.

How to Panel an Attic Ceiling

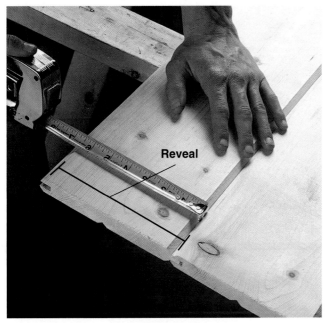

1 To plan your layout, first measure the reveal of the boards—the exposed surface when they are installed. Fit two pieces together and measure from the bottom edge of the upper board to the bottom edge of the lower board. Calculate the number of boards needed to cover one side of the ceiling by dividing the reveal dimension into the overall distance between the top of one wall and the peak.

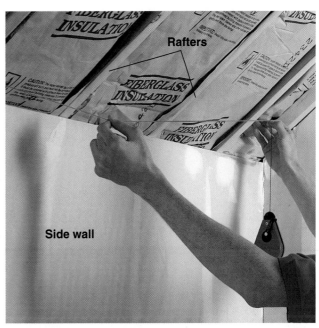

2 Use the calculation from step 1 to make a control line indicating the top of the first row of panels. At both ends of the ceiling, measure down from the peak an equal distance, and make a mark to represent the top (tongue) edges of the starter boards. Snap a chalk line through the marks.

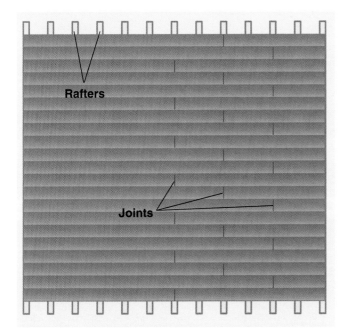

3 If the boards aren't long enough to span the entire ceiling, plan the locations of the joints. Staggering the joints in a three-step pattern will make them less conspicuous. Note that each joint must fall over the middle of a rafter. For best appearance, select boards of similar coloring and grain for each row.

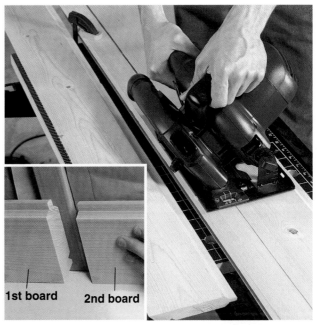

4 Rip the first starter board to width by bevel-cutting the bottom (grooved) edge. If the starter row will have joints, cut the board to length using a 30° bevel cut on the joint-end only. Two beveled ends joined together form a *scarf* joint (inset), which is less noticeable than a butt joint. If the board spans the ceiling, square-cut both ends.

(continued next page)

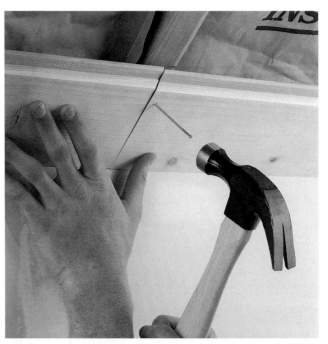

5 Position the first starter board so the grooved (or cut) edge butts against the side wall and the tongue is aligned with the control line. Leave a ⅛" gap between the square board end and the end wall. Fasten the board by nailing through its face about 1" from the grooved edge and into the rafters. Then, blind-nail through the base of the tongue into each rafter, angling the nail backwards at 45°. Drive the nail heads beneath the wood surface, using a nail set.

6 Cut and install any remaining boards in the starter row one at a time, making sure the scarf joints fit together tightly. At each scarf joint, drive two nails through the face of the top board, angling the nail to capture the end of the board behind it. If necessary, predrill the nail holes to prevent splitting.

7 Cut the first board for the next row, then fit its grooved edge over the tongue of the board in the starter row. Use a hammer and a scrap piece of paneling to drive downward on the tongue edge, seating the grooved edge over the tongue of the starter board. Fasten the second row of boards with blind-nails only.

8 As you install successive rows, measure down from the peak to make sure the rows remain parallel to the peak. Correct any misalignment by adjusting the tongue-and-groove joint slightly with each row. You can also snap additional control lines to help align the rows.

9 Rip the boards for the last row to width, beveling the top edges so they fit flush against the ridge board. Face nail the boards in place. Install paneling on the other side of the ceiling, then cut and install the final row of panels to form a closed joint under the ridge board (inset).

10 Install trim molding along walls, at joints around obstacles, and along inside and outside corners, if desired. (Select-grade 1 × 2 works well as trim along walls.) Where necessary, bevel the back edges of the trim or miter-cut the ends to accommodate the slope of the ceiling.

Tips for Paneling an Attic Ceiling

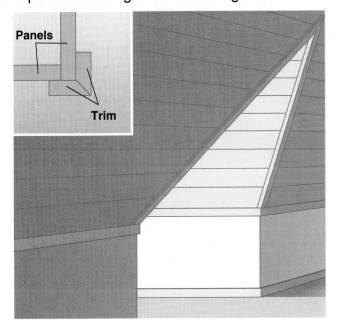

Use mitered trim to cover joints where panels meet at outside corners. Dormers and other attic elements create opposing ceiling angles that can be difficult to panel around. It may be easier to butt the panels together and hide the butt joints with custom-cut trim. The trim also makes a nice transition between angles.

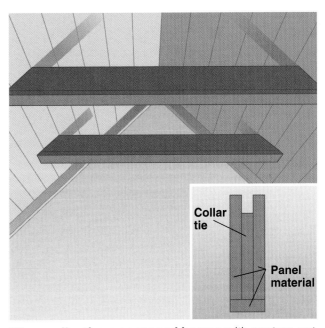

Wrap collar ties or exposed beams with custom-cut panels. Install the paneling on the ceiling first. Then, rip-cut panels to the desired width. You may want to include a tongue-and-groove joint as part of the trim detail. Angle-cut the ends of the trim so it fits tight to the ceiling panels.

Installing Doors & Windows

In simple terms, installing a standard window or prehung door is merely a matter of positioning the unit in the framed opening, adjusting it so that it's plumb, square, and level, then fastening it to the framing. Making the adjustments can be a little tricky, and there are wall surfaces to consider, but the basic procedure is fairly straightforward—and well within the skill level of most do-it-yourselfers.

You should hang doors after the wallboard or other finish material is in place. The jambs on most prehung doors are the same width as a 2 × 4 framed wall with a layer of ½" wallboard on each side, and having the wallboard in place makes it easier to center the door jambs in the opening so they end up flush with the wall on both sides. Windows also should be installed with the jambs flush with the wall surface, but there are advantages to installing windows early in a project. You may want the added natural light from the windows as you work, or it may be convenient to gain access through a new window.

Skylights essentially are windows in roofs, and framing and installing skylights is similar in many ways to framing and installing standard windows. This section includes a project that shows you how to add a new skylight from start to finish, including building the frame, installing the unit, and adding the all-important flashing, which prevents leaking.

As you read through these projects, keep in mind that there are many types of windows and skylights, as well as exterior wall finishes. Not all of the steps shown in these installation projects will apply to your situation. Therefore, it's important to follow manufacturer's instructions carefully.

After your windows and doors are in place and you've made sure they operate properly, install the interior trim, or *casing*, to complete the project. Most door and window units do not come with casing; it's up to you to select a molding that looks good with the window or door and matches or complements other trim in the room. A good lumber yard or home center will have a variety of casing in several wood species and manufactured materials.

Top jamb

Latch-side jamb

Hinge-side jamb

Installing a Prehung Interior Door

Prehung doors come as single units with the door already hung on hinges attached to a factory-built door frame. To secure the unit during shipping, most prehung doors are nailed shut with a couple of duplex nails driven through the jambs and into the door edge. When you're ready to install the door, lean the unit against the wall near the opening, and remove those nails.

The key to installing doors is to plumb and fasten the hinge-side jamb first. After that's in place, you can use the door to position the top and latch-side jambs, by checking the *reveal*— the gap between the closed door and the jamb.

Standard prehung doors have 4½"-wide jambs and are sized to fit walls with 2 × 4 construction and ½" wallboard. If you have thicker walls, you can special-order a door to match, or you can add jamb extensions to a standard-size door.

Everything You Need:

Tools: 4-ft. level, nail set, handsaw.

Materials: Prehung door unit, wood shims, 8d casing nails.

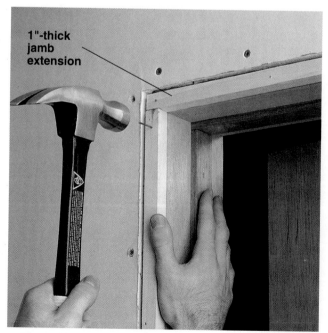

1"-thick jamb extension

If your walls are built with 2 × 6 studs, you'll need to extend the jambs by attaching 1" thick wood strips to the jamb edges on both sides. Use glue and 4d casing nails to attach these extensions to the jambs.

How to Install a Prehung Interior Door

1 Set the door unit into the framed opening so the jamb edges are flush with the wall surfaces and the unit is centered from side to side. Using a level, adjust the unit so the hinge-side jamb is plumb.

2 Starting near the top hinge, insert pairs of shims driven from opposite directions into the gap between the framing and the jamb, sliding in the shims until they are snug. Check the jamb to make sure it remains plumb and does not bow inward. Install shims near each hinge.

3 Anchor the hinge-side jamb with 8d casing nails driven through the jamb and shims and into the framing. Drive nails only at the shim locations.

4 Insert pairs of shims into the gap between the framing members and the top jamb and latch-side jamb, aligning them roughly with the hinge-side shims. With the door closed, adjust the shims so the reveal is 1/16"-1/8" wide. Drive casing nails through the jambs and shims and into the framing members.

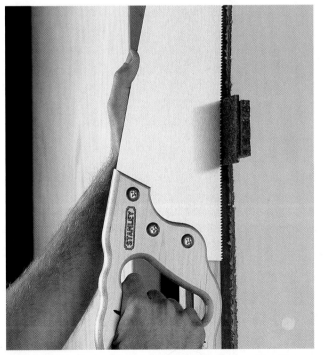

5 Set all nails below the surface of the wood with a nail set, then cut off the shims flush with the wall surface, using a handsaw or utility knife. Hold the saw vertically to prevent damage to the door jamb or wall. See pages 132 to 133 to install the door casing.

Installing Windows

If you're installing a window in an attic wall or the framed wall of a walkout basement, you'll probably have to remove the exterior wall sheathing and finish material to clear the window opening. The basic techniques for removing wood siding are shown here. If your house has stucco, brick, or aluminum, vinyl, or other type of siding, consult the siding manufacturer or a remodeling professional for help with removal.

Also note that this installation project involves a wood-frame window and a wood-frame wall. Other window types may require different installation methods, as will installing a window in an exposed-masonry wall.

Everything You Need:

Tools: Drill, chalk line, circular saw, reciprocating saw, 2-ft. level, chisel, stapler, nail set, utility knife, caulk gun.

Materials: 10d galvanized casing nails, 8d casing nails, 1 × 4, cedar shims, building paper, drip edge, unfaced fiberglass insulation, silicone caulk.

How to Remove Wood Siding

1 From inside, drill through the wall at the corners of the framed opening. Push casing nails through the holes to mark their locations. For round-top windows, drill several holes around the curved outline.

2 Measure the distance between the nails on the outside of the wall to make sure the dimensions are accurate. Mark the cutting lines with a chalk line stretched between the nails. Push the nails back through the wall.

3 Tack a straight 1 x 4 to the wall so its edge is flush against the inside of one of the cutting lines. Drive the nails flush with the surface. Set the blade depth on a circular saw to cut through only the siding, taking into account the thickness of the 1 x 4. NOTE: Use an old saw blade or a remodeling blade, as you're likely to hit nails as you cut through the siding.

4 Rest the saw on the 1 x 4, and cut along the chalk line, using the edge of the board as a guide. Stop the cut about 1" from each corner to avoid cutting into the framing. Reposition the board, and make the remaining cuts. Be sure to wear safety goggles while cutting through siding.

Variation: For round-top windows, make curved cuts, using a reciprocating saw or jig saw. Move the saw slowly to ensure smooth cuts.

5 Complete the cuts at the corners with a reciprocating saw or jig saw, being careful not to cut into the framing.

6 Remove the cut-out wall section. You may want to remove the siding pieces from the sheathing and save them for future use.

How to Install a Window (in a wood frame)

Mullion post

1 Set the window into the frame from the outside. Slide tapered cedar shims (and small wood blocks, if necessary) under the side jambs and mullion post so that the window is centered in the opening from side to side and top to bottom. Use the level to make sure the window is perfectly plumb and level, adjusting the shims as needed.

Brick molding

2 Trace the outline of the brick molding onto the wood siding. Remove the window, and cut the siding along the outline just down to the sheathing, using a reciprocating saw held at a low angle (inset). For straight cuts, you can use a circular saw set to the depth of the siding (see page 123), then finish the cuts at the corners with a chisel.

3 Cut 8"-wide strips of building paper and slide them behind the siding and around the entire window frame, then staple them in place. Cut a length of drip edge to fit over the top of the window, and fit its back flange between the siding and sheathing. Use flexible drip edge for round-top windows and rigid drip edge for straight-top units.

4 Reset the window and push the brick molding tight against the sheathing. Use the level to make sure the window is plumb and level, and adjust the shims, if necessary. Drive a 10d galvanized casing nail through the brick molding and into the frame at each corner.

5 From inside, install flat pairs of shims between the window jambs and the frame, spaced every 12". The shims should be snug but not so tight that they bow the jambs. Use a level to check for bowing, then open and close the window to make sure it operates smoothly.

6 At each shim location, drill a pilot hole and drive an 8d casing nail through the jamb and into the frame. Set the nails with a nail set. Trim the shims flush to the frame using a utility knife or a handsaw, then fill the gaps behind the jambs with loosely packed fiberglass insulation.

7 From outside, drive 10d galvanized casing nails, spaced every 12", through the brick molding and into the frame. Set all nails with a nail set. Apply silicone caulk around the entire perimeter where the brick molding meets the siding. Fill all nail holes with caulk.

Installation Variation: Masonry Clips

Use metal masonry clips when the brick molding on a window cannot be nailed because it rests against a masonry surface. The masonry clips hook into precut grooves in the window jambs (above, left) and are attached to the jambs with screws. After setting the window in the frame, bend the masonry clips around the framing members and anchor them with screws (above, right). NOTE: Masonry clips also can be used in ordinary lap siding installations if you want to avoid making nail holes in the surface of the brick molding.

Installing a Skylight

A skylight is a great addition to a finished attic. Depending on the model you choose and where you place it, a skylight can offer warmth in the winter, cooling ventilation in the summer, and a lofty view of the sky or the treetops around your house. And of course, all skylights provide a lot of natural light.

Because a skylight lets in so much light, the sizing and placement of the unit are important considerations. A skylight that's too big (or using too many of them) can quickly overheat a space, especially in an attic. For the same reason, it's often best to position a skylight away from the day's brightest sun. Other ways to avoid overheating include choosing a model with tinted glazing or a low solar-heat-gain coefficient (between .30 and .50), or simply shading the skylight during the hottest hours of the day.

Some attics offer little space for windows and, thus, limited sources of fresh air, so you may want to spend a little more on your skylight and get an operable model that opens and closes. These are good for venting warm air that would otherwise get trapped in the attic, and they help draw cooler air from the floors below.

A skylight frame is similar to a standard window frame (see page 68). It has a header and sill, like a window frame, but has *king rafters*, rather than king studs. Skylight frames also have *trimmers* that define the sides of the rough opening. Refer to the manufacturer's instructions to determine what size to make the opening for your skylight.

With standard rafter-frame roof construction, you can safely cut into one or two rafters, as long as you permanently support the cut rafters, as shown in this project. If your skylight requires alteration of more than two rafters, or if your roofing is made with unusually heavy material, such as clay tile or slate, consult an architect or engineer before starting the project.

Today's good-quality skylight units are unlikely to leak, but a skylight is only as leakproof as its installation: Follow the manufacturer's instructions, and install the flashing meticulously, as it will last a lot longer than any sealant.

Everything You Need:

Tools: 4-ft. level, circular saw, drill, combination square, reciprocating saw, pry bar, chalk line, stapler, caulk gun, utility knife, tin snips.

Materials: 2 × lumber, 16d and 10d common nails, 1 × 4, building paper, roofing cement, skylight flashing, 2", 1¼", and ¾" roofing nails.

How to Install a Skylight

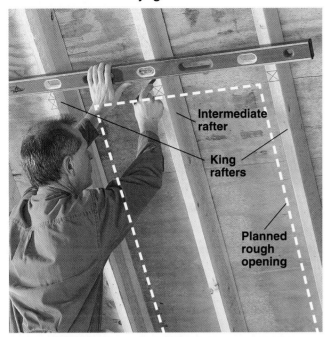

1 Use the first rafter on each side of the planned rough opening to serve as a king rafter. Measure and mark where the double header and sill will fit against the king rafters. Then, use a level as a straightedge to extend the marks across the intermediate rafter.

2 Brace the intermediate rafter by installing two 2 × 4s between the rafter and the attic floor. Position the braces just above the header marks and just below the sill marks. Secure them temporarily to the rafter and subfloor with screws.

3 Reinforce each king rafter by attaching a full-length "sister" rafter against its outside face. Cut the sister rafters from the same size of lumber as the existing rafters, matching the lengths and end cuts exactly. Work each sister rafter into position, flush against the outside face of the king rafters, then nail the sisters to the kings with pairs of 10d common nails, spaced 12" apart.

4 Use a combination square to transfer the sill and header marks across the face of the intermediate rafter, then cut along the outermost lines with a reciprocating saw. Do not cut into the roof sheathing. Carefully remove the cut-out section with a pry bar. The remaining rafter portions will serve as cripple rafters.

(continued next page)

5 Build a double header and double sill to fit snugly between the king rafters, using 2 × lumber that is the same size as the rafters. Nail the header pieces together using pairs of 10d nails, spaced 6" apart.

Cripple rafter

6 Install the header and sill, anchoring them to the king rafters and cripple rafters with 16d common nails. Make sure the ends of the header and sill are aligned with the appropriate marks on the king rafters.

Trimmers

7 If your skylight unit is narrower than the opening between the king studs, measure and make marks for the trimmers: They should be centered in the opening and spaced according to the manufacturer's specifications. Cut the trimmers from the same 2 × lumber used for the rest of the frame, and nail them in place with 10d common nails.

8 When the skylight frame is complete, remove the 2 × 4 rafter braces. Then, mark the opening for the roof cutout by driving a screw through the sheathing at each corner of the frame.

9 From the roof, measure between the screws to make sure the rough opening dimensions are accurate. Snap chalk lines on the shingles between the screws to mark the rough opening, then remove the screws.

10 Tack a straight 1 × 4 to the roof aligned with the inside edge of one chalk line. Make sure the nail heads are flush with the surface of the board.

11 Cut through the shingles and sheathing along the chalk line, using a circular saw and an old blade or a remodeling blade. Rest the saw foot on the 1 × 4, and use the edge of the board as a guide. Reposition the 1 × 4, and cut along the remaining lines. Remove the cut-out roof section.

12 Remove shingles around the rough opening with a flat pry bar, exposing at least 9" of building paper on all sides of the opening. Remove entire shingles, rather than cutting them.

(continued next page)

13 Cut strips of building paper and slide them between the shingles and existing building paper. Wrap the paper around so that it covers the faces of the framing members, and staple it in place.

Nailing flange

14 Spread a 5"-wide layer of roofing cement around the roof opening. Set the skylight into the opening so that the nailing flange rests on the roof. Adjust the unit so that it sits squarely in the opening.

15 Nail through the nailing flange and into the sheathing and framing members with 2" galvanized roofing nails spaced every 6". NOTE: If your skylight uses L-shaped brackets instead of a nailing flange, follow the manufacturer's instructions.

Adhesive strip

16 Patch in shingles up to the bottom edge of the skylight unit. Attach the shingles with 1¼" roofing nails driven just below the adhesive strip. If necessary, cut the shingles with a utility knife so that they fit against the bottom of the skylight.

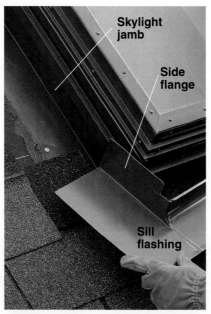

Skylight jamb

Side flange

Sill flashing

17 Spread roofing cement on the bottom edge of the sill flashing, then fit the flashing around the bottom of the unit. Attach the flashing by driving ¾" galvanized roofing nails through the vertical side flange (near the top of the flashing) and into the skylight jambs.

Step flashing

5" overlap

Drip edge

18 Spread roofing cement on the bottom of a piece of step flashing, then slide the flashing under the drip edge on one side of the skylight. The step flashing should overlap the sill flashing by 5". Press the step flashing down to bond it. Do the same on the opposite side of the skylight.

19 Patch in the next row of shingles on each side of the skylight, following the existing shingle pattern. Drive a 1¼" roofing nail through each shingle and the step flashing and into the sheathing. Drive additional nails just above the notches in the shingles.

20 Continue applying alternate rows of step flashing and shingles, using roofing cement and roofing nails. Each piece of flashing should overlap the preceding piece by 5".

21 At the top of the skylight, cut and bend the last piece of step flashing on each side, so the vertical flange wraps around the corner of the skylight. Patch in the next row of shingles.

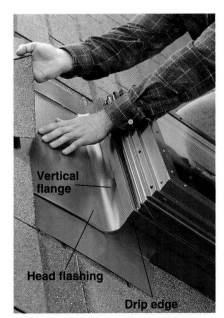

22 Spread roofing cement on the bottom of the head flashing, to bond it to the roof. Position the flashing against the top of the skylight so the vertical flange fits under the drip edge and the horizontal flange fits under the shingles above the skylight.

23 Fill in the remaining shingles, cutting them to fit, if necessary. Attach the shingles with roofing nails driven just above the notches.

24 Apply a continuous bead of roofing cement along the joint between the shingles and skylight. Finish the interior of the framed opening as desired.

Installing Door & Window Casing

Casing is the decorative molding that covers the gaps around the edges of door and window jambs. You can find casing in almost any style and in many different materials, including pine, hardwoods, and manufactured materials. If you'll be painting wood casing, use *finger-jointed* material, which is made from small pieces of pine assembled with finger joints: It's less expensive than standard casing, and you can't tell the difference once it's painted.

In most cases, it's easier to paint the walls before you install the casing. You can also save time by applying primer to casing you'll be painting, or by staining the casing before cutting or installing it. After it's installed, paint the casing or apply touch-up stain to cover any bare wood.

To ensure precise miter cuts that make tight joints, use a power miter saw, if you have one; otherwise, make cuts with a miter box and backsaw.

How to Install Casing

1 On the front edge of each jamb, mark a setback line to indicate the inside edge of the casing. The typical setback is about ⅛". You can set back your molding as much as you'd like—just make sure the distance is equal on all jambs. Use a straightedge to mark the lines just at the corners, or extend them along the entire length of the jambs.

Everything You Need:

Tools: Straightedge, power miter saw or miter box and backsaw, drill, nail set.

Materials: Casing, 6d and 4d finish nails, wood putty.

2 Place a length of casing along one side jamb, flush with the setback line. At the top and bottom of the molding, mark the points where the horizontal and vertical setback lines meet. (With doors, mark the top ends only.)

3 Make 45° miter cuts on the ends of the moldings. Measure and cut the other vertical molding piece, using the same methods.

4 Tack each vertical piece in place with two 4d finish nails driven through the casing and into the jamb. Drill pilot holes for the nails to prevent splitting. Do not drive the nails flush at this step.

5 Measure between the vertical pieces, and cut the top and bottom pieces to length, making 45° cuts on the ends. If the joints don't fit well, move the molding pieces slightly, or make new cuts. When all of the pieces fit well, drill pilot holes and attach them to the jambs with 4d finish nails, spacing the nails every 12"-16". Then drive 6d finish nails through the casing near the outer edge and into the wall framing.

6 Lock-nail the corner joints by drilling a pilot hole and driving a 4d finish nail through each corner, as shown. Drive all nail heads below the wood surface, using a nail set, then fill the nail holes with wood putty.

Projects

In This Section:

Wet Bar

A wet bar typically consists of a small set of cabinets, a countertop, and a sink—a convenient setup for serving drinks or snacks. But by expanding on this basic theme, you can build a bar that brings several amenities of a kitchen right into your new family room or home theater. In addition to providing a place to serve drinks, the new bar will be great for microwaving popcorn or grabbing a cold drink during halftime or movie intermissions.

This project shows you how to build a wet bar that includes a countertop with plenty of room for appliances (and a nearby GFCI receptacle), an under-counter refrigerator/freezer, four full-size cabinets, and a set of elegant glass shelves. At 2 × 6½ ft., the bar can fit easily into a corner or along a wall. Low-voltage halogen lights placed under the cabinets provide task lighting while additional lights above accent the bar without brightening the room too much.

To begin planning the project, review *Making Preparations,* on pages 136-137. This gives you

an overview of the framing requirements and the plumbing and wiring rough-ins needed for the bar. Be aware that the project involves several plumbing connections, as well as some basic wiring. If you aren't familiar with these procedures, consult good books on the subjects, or hire a professional to complete the rough-ins and make the final connections.

After you've made the preparations, follow the step-by-step instructions to install the cabinets, shelves, countertop, and sink, then complete the plumbing and wiring connections, and install the cabinet lights.

Careful placement of the bar will help the project go more smoothly. Wiring can go almost anywhere, but plumbing requires more consideration: To save time and money, locate the bar as close as possible to existing plumbing lines. Also, the fixtures and configurations in this project may not meet code requirements in your area, so have your project plans reviewed by a local building inspector before you start.

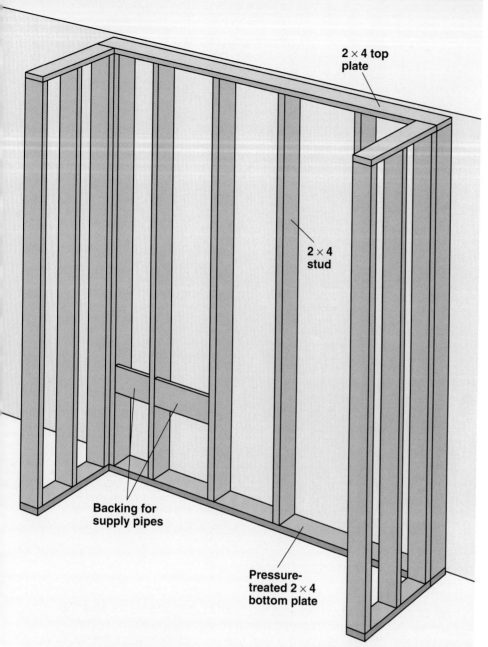

2 × 4 top plate

2 × 4 stud

Backing for supply pipes

Pressure-treated 2 × 4 bottom plate

crete floor to run the drain line for the sink (see pages 79-80).

You'll also need to know the dimensions of the fixtures going into the wet bar so you can determine the size of the frame. Confirm with the manufacturers the exact dimensions of the cabinets, appliances, fixtures, and countertop you've chosen. Be sure to add the thickness of the wallboard when sizing the frame.

Building the frame itself is simple (see drawing, left). Construct standard 2 × 4 partition walls, with single bottom and top plates, using 16"-on-center spacing. Use pressure-treated lumber for the bottom plates if the bar is in the basement. (See pages 60-63 for help with basic wall framing.)

It's very important that the framing of the wet bar walls be square: The side walls must be perpendicular to the back wall and parallel to each other. This affects how well the cabinets and countertop fit. Since the side walls of the bar are short, you can use a framing square to check them.

The wet bar in this project has a 12" space above the wall cabinets, which is typical with standard cabinets installed under 8-ft.-high ceilings. You can leave this space open and use it for accent lighting or as a display shelf, or enclose the space with a framed soffit, as is common in most kitchens.

After the frame is built, complete the plumbing and electrical rough-ins (see drawing, page 137). First, install the drain and vent pipes for the bar sink. Run 1½" drain pipe from the sink location to the main stack or other waste/vent pipe. In a basement, this may require cutting into and breaking up a section of the concrete floor. Set the height of the drain stub-out as required by local code (typically 19" above the floor). Remember that most horizontal drain runs must have a downward slope of ¼" per foot.

According to most codes, sinks must be ventilated within 3½ ft. of the fixture's drain trap. If the

Making Preparations

NOTE: Always shut off the water supply before working with plumbing. Shut off electrical power at the main service panel and test for power with a circuit tester before doing any electrical work.

The frame requirements for your wet bar depend upon its location. If the back of the bar is set against a masonry wall, the bar will need a framed back wall for holding plumbing and wiring. If the bar is set against an existing framed wall, you may be able to run the service lines through that framing. If the wall is load-bearing, be sure to follow local code requirements for notching and boring into framing.

Before you start the framing, you'll need to plan the rough-ins. If the bar is going in the basement, you may have to break up a portion of the con-

waste/vent pipe is within this limit, it can serve as both drain and vent for the sink. Otherwise, you'll need a 1½" vent pipe that extends up and over to the nearest acceptable vent. The new vent pipe must extend upward a minimum of 6" above the flood level of the sink before turning to begin a horizontal run.

To provide hot and cold water to the sink, tap into the nearest water distribution lines with ¾ × ½" reducing T-fittings. Run ½" supply pipes from the fittings to the sink location. Complete the supply stub-outs with an angle stop shutoff valve on each supply pipe. The stub-outs should be spaced about 8" apart.

Install five electrical boxes: one for a single-pole switch, centered 45" above the floor; one for the refrigerator receptacle, centered 12" above the floor; one for the over-counter GFCI receptacle; and one for each cable leading to the low-voltage lighting transformers, located just above the tops of the wall cabinets.

Next, run cable to the boxes. Lighting for the bar is supplied by one 14/2 cable that can be branched from an existing 15-amp lighting circuit. Run the cable to the box for the switch, then run a branch cable from the switch box to the box for the first transformer. Run another cable between the transformer boxes.

To prevent circuit trippings that would shut off the refrigerator, wire the two receptacles on a dedicated 20-amp circuit. Run 12/2 cable from the service panel to the GFCI receptacle box, then add a branch cable leading to the box for the standard 20-amp receptacle.

Install metal protector plates where pipes and cables pass through framing. After the framing and rough-ins have been inspected and approved, cover the walls and ceiling of the bar with ½" wallboard. Tape and finish the wallboard so the surfaces are completely smooth and flat. Apply primer, then paint the walls and ceiling the color of your choice.

Complete the wiring connections for all devices except the low-voltage lights (see page 141). Install each device in its electrical box, and attach the coverplate.

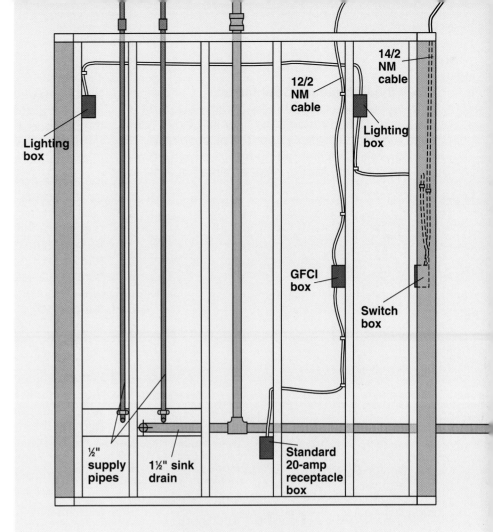

Everything You Need:

Tools: 4-ft. and 2-ft. level, chisel, drill, hole saw, utility knife, nail set, circular saw, compass, belt sander, jig saw and laminate blade, caulk gun, channel-type pliers, framing square, wallboard finishing tools, combination tool (for wiring).

Materials: 2 × 4 lumber, 16d common nails, 1½" drain pipe and fittings, ¾ × ½" reducing T-fittings, ½" copper pipe, shutoff valves, escutcheons, electrical boxes, 12/2 and 14/2 NM cable, 20-amp GFCI receptacle, 20-amp receptacle, 15-amp single-pole switch, low-voltage lighting kit, wire connectors, coverplates w/knockouts, cable clamps, ½" wallboard, wallboard finishing materials, primer, paint, cabinets, duct tape, 2½" sheet metal screws, shelf brackets, glass shelves, cedar shims, construction adhesive, toe-kick molding, finish nails, ¾" plywood, wallboard screws, masking tape, silicone caulk, bar sink, faucet, sink-drain assembly, supply tubes.

(continued next page)

Install the Cabinets & Countertop

Draw layout lines for both sets of cabinets. First, use a level to determine if the floor is even. If not, make a mark on the wall near the high point of the floor. Measure straight up from the high point and make a mark for the base cabinets at 34½".

1 Measure up from the floor's high point, and draw level lines for the tops of both sets of cabinets.

Make a mark for the wall cabinets at 84". Use the level to draw level lines through each of these marks to indicate the top edges of all four cabinets **(photo 1)**. Also mark the stud locations just above each level line.

Install the coverplates onto the lighting-cable boxes, feeding the cable ends through the clamps in the coverplates and clamping them in place. Prepare the wall cabinets by installing the transformers and fixture wires. Mount one transformer on the top of each wall cabinet with screws. Create a recess for the fixture wires by chiseling a small channel into the back of the support strips at the top and bottom of each wall cabinet. Connect the fixture wires to the transformer, lay them in the channels, and hold them in place with tape **(photo 2)**.

Have a helper position one wall cabinet against the back and side walls, aligning its top edge with the upper layout line. Drill pilot holes through the hanging strips inside the cabinet and into the wall studs. Fasten the cabinet to the wall with 2½" sheet metal screws **(photo 3)**. Install the remaining wall cabinet against the opposite side wall.

Measure up from the bottom edge on the inside face of each wall cabinet, and make light pencil marks to indicate the height of each shelf bracket. Use a level to make sure the marks are aligned and level. Drill holes for the bracket posts and install the brackets **(photo 4)**. Measure between the brackets to determine the

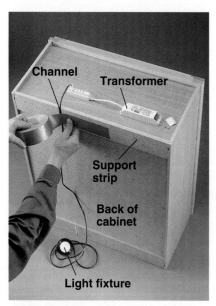

2 Lay the fixture wire into the channels on the back of each wall cabinet, and secure them with duct tape.

3 Set each wall cabinet against the back and side walls, and attach it with screws.

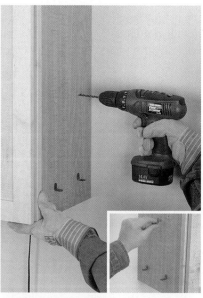

4 Drill holes to accept the posts of the shelf brackets, then push the brackets into place.

length of the glass shelves. Have the shelves cut about ⅛" short so that you can install them easily.

To set the sink base cabinet, measure the locations of the plumbing stub-outs and transfer the measurements to the back panel of the cabinet. Cut the holes for the stub-outs, using a drill and hole saw **(photo 5).** If necessary, use a jig saw to cut the hole for the drain stub-out.

Set the sink base cabinet in place. Where necessary, slide tapered cedar shims under the cabinet's bottom edges until the cabinet is aligned with the layout line and is perfectly plumb from front to back **(photo 6).** Apply a small amount of construction adhesive to the shims to hold them in place. Fasten the cabinet to the wall studs, as with the wall cabinets. Install the remaining cabinet against the opposite side wall.

When the adhesive on the shims has dried, cut off the shims flush with the cabinets, using a utility knife. Install the toe-kick molding supplied by the manufacturer. Position the molding flush along the floor, with the ends flush with the cabinet sides. Drill pilot holes through the toe-kicks, and fasten them to cabinets with finish nails **(photo 7).** Set the nails with a nail set.

Install a ¾"-thick × 2"-wide plywood support cleat to the back wall between the base cabinets, keeping the cleat ¾" above the layout line. Then, attach ¾"-thick × 2"-wide plywood buildup strips to the front and back edges of the cabinets. The strips keep the bottom of the countertop's front edge level with the top of the cabinets so they don't hang over the drawer fronts. Fasten the strips flush with the outside edges of the cabinet, using wallboard screws driven through pilot holes **(photo 8).**

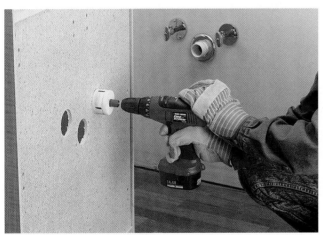

5 Cut holes through the back panel of the sink base cabinet for plumbing lines, using a hole saw.

6 Shim under the sink base cabinet so that it is perfectly plumb and is aligned with the layout line.

7 Trim the shims, and install the toe-kick molding with finish nails driven through pilot holes.

Buildup strip

Support cleat

8 Install a plywood support cleat and buildup strips to provide support for the countertop.

(continued next page)

Set the countertop onto the cabinets. Check to see how the backsplash meets the back wall: If there are any gaps over ¹⁄₁₆", scribe the backsplash with a compass. Set the compass to the width of the widest gap, then run it along the wall to transfer the wall contours onto the backsplash **(photo 9).** Remove the countertop and sand the edge of the backsplash down to the scribed line. Use a belt sander, holding it parallel to the backsplash to prevent chipping **(photo 10).**

Make the sink cutout, using the sink template. Place strips of masking tape on the countertop, then trace around the template with a pencil. Apply tape to the foot of a jig saw to prevent

scratching. Drill a starter hole just inside the cutting line, then complete the cutout with the saw. Use a laminate blade or a down-cutting blade, and cut from the finished side of the countertop **(photo 11).** After cutting around each corner, drive an angled screw into the edge of the cutout piece, to keep the piece from falling before the cut is complete, which could chip the laminate.

Reset the countertop, and secure it in place by driving wallboard screws up through the fastening brackets in the cabinet corners (and the buildup strips) and into the particleboard core of the countertop **(photo 12).** Make sure the screws are not long enough to puncture the laminate

9 *Set the countertop. If necessary, scribe the backsplash with a compass.*

10 *Sand the backsplash so it fits tight to the back wall.*

11 *Draw the sink cutout onto the countertop, then make the cut with a jigsaw.*

Fastening bracket

12 *Secure the countertop through the cabinet brackets*

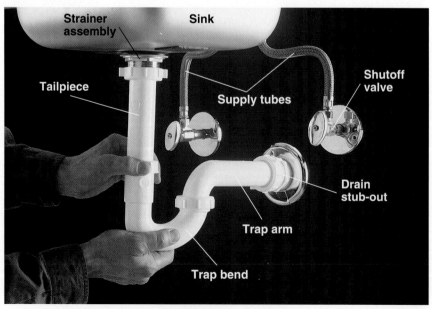

Strainer assembly · Sink · Tailpiece · Supply tubes · Shutoff valve · Drain stub-out · Trap arm · Trap bend

13 *Install the sink in the countertop, connect the water supply tubes to the faucet, and complete the drain assembly.*

surface. Complete the countertop installation by sealing all joints along the wall with a thin bead of silicone caulk.

Install the Sink & Faucet

Install the faucet, following the manufacturer's instructions. Attach the sink strainer assembly to the sink, then install the sink in the countertop, following the manufacturer's instructions. Be sure to include a watertight seal under the sink rim, using caulk or plumber's putty. Connect flexible supply tubes between the faucet tailpieces and the appropriate shutoff valves. Tighten the connecting nuts with channel-type pliers.

To complete the drain hookup, attach a drain tailpiece to the strainer, then attach a trap arm to the drain stub-out, making the connection with a threaded coupling and a slip washer and nut. Slide the long end of a trap bend (P-trap) onto the tailpiece until the short end meets the opening of the trap arm. Secure the pieces together with slip washers and nuts. Hand-tighten the nuts **(photo 13).**

Set the Shelves & Lighting Fixtures

Install the glass shelves. Connect the circuit cables to the lighting transformers, following the manufacturer's instructions. With the lights on, position the light fixtures in the desired locations **(photo 14).** Turn off the lights, and attach them to the cabinets with screws. Finally, staple the fixture wires to the bottoms of the cabinets.

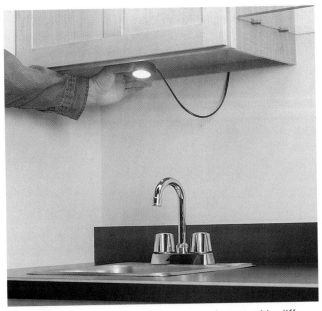

14 *Turn on the lights and experiment with different positions to find the best locations.*

Making the Electrical Connections

NOTE: Turn off the power at the main service panel, and use a circuit tester to confirm the power is off before working with electrical cables.

Connect the GFCI receptacle so that it protects itself but not the receptacle for the refrigerator. Pigtail the hot wires to the HOT LINE terminal, and pigtail the neutral wires to the WHITE LINE terminal. Pigtail the grounding wires to the GFCI's grounding screw **(photo A).**

Connect the 20-amp refrigerator receptacle to the wires from the branch cable **(photo B).**

Install the single-pole switch with middle-of-run wiring configuration. Attach one hot wire to each screw terminal, and join the neutral wires together with a wire connector **(photo C).** If the switch has a grounding screw, pigtail the ground wires to the grounding screw. If there's no grounding screw, join the two grounding wires with a wire connector.

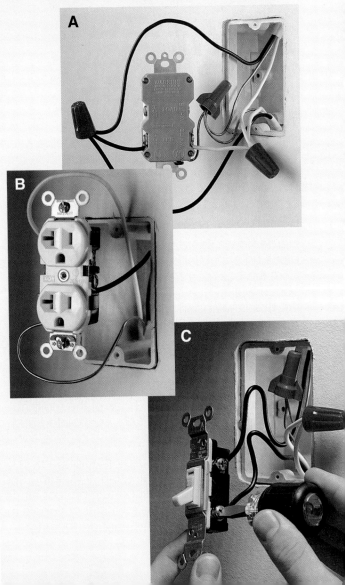

Light Boxes

These light boxes can supply plenty of light to a finished space without giving up valuable headroom or floor area. An even greater feature is that the boxes are custom-made: You can build them with 2-, 4-, or 6-ft. light fixtures, and you can add a light box anywhere there's an open area between joists.

Here's how a light box is made: Two pieces of blocking are installed between two floor joists to form the box (see page 143). The wiring is run from a wall switch into the box, then the inside of the box is wrapped with ¼" wallboard. After the wallboard is finished and painted, one fluorescent light fixture is installed on each long side of the box, and the wiring connections are made. Then, a piece of crown molding and a spacer are cut to length to fit under each fixture. Reflective tape is applied to the back of the molding, and the molding and spacers are painted and fastened to the box sides.

Part of the planning for building a light box is finding an effective combination of molding and spacer pieces. The molding must project far enough from the box side so that it conceals the fixture from view but allows enough room for

changing the lamp. A spacer cut from standard 2 × lumber combined with a 5" or 6" crown molding should provide the desired effect. Another option is to make boxes without using spacers (see page 145).

The wiring diagrams on page 143 show you a fixture connection and the basic wiring layout for multiple light boxes. If you're not familiar with basic wiring techniques and installation, hire an electrician to rough-in the wiring and make the final connections for your light boxes. Be sure to have all of the electrical work approved by a building inspector.

Everything You Need:

Tools: Combination square, circular saw, drill, wallboard knives, paintbrush, nail set, caulk gun.

Materials: 2 × lumber, 3" wallboard screws, 14/2 NM cable, cable staples, single-pole light switch, electrical box, wire connectors, fluorescent light fixtures, ¼" wallboard, corner bead, wallboard tape & compound, paint, crown molding, foil duct tape, finish nails, caulk, wood putty.

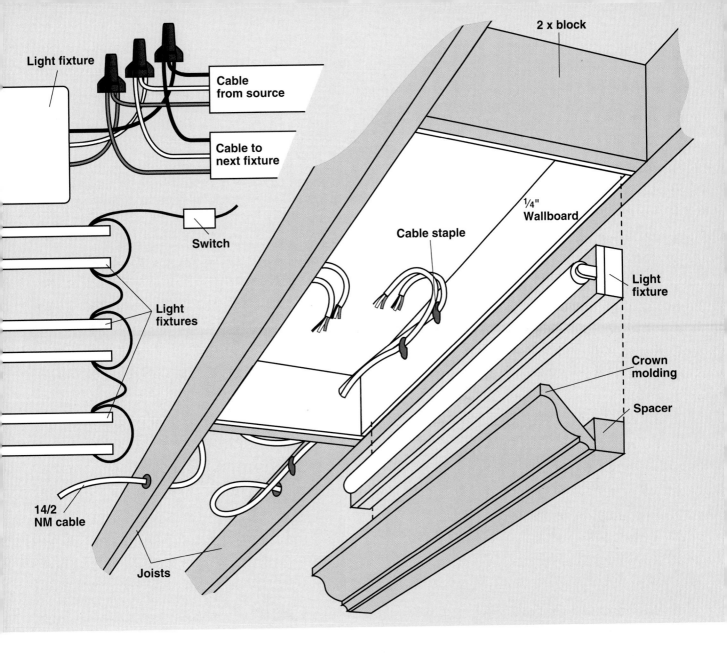

Light fixture

Cable from source

Cable to next fixture

2 x block

Switch

¼" **Wallboard**

Cable staple

Light fixtures

Light fixture

Crown molding

Spacer

14/2 NM cable

Joists

Build the Box Frames & Run the Wiring

Measure from a side wall and mark the locations of the boxes. Make Xs on the bottom edges of the joists to indicate the blocks of the frame. The inside of the frame should be about 2" longer than the light fixtures. Use a combination square to extend the layout lines onto the faces of joists. Cut each block to length so it fits snugly between the two joists, using the same size lumber as the joists. Set the blocks into place, aligning them with the layout lines and keeping the bottom edges flush with the joists. Secure the blocks with 3" wallboard screws driven through the faces of the joists and into the blocks **(photo 1).** Drill ⅝" holes through the end blocks and run the wiring for the boxes (see diagram, above).

Finish the Boxes & Install the Fixtures

Cover all of the surfaces inside the box with ¼" wallboard. Complete the wallboard installation

1 *Fit the blocks between the joists and secure them with screws to form the ends of the box frames.*

(continued next page)

143

over the main ceiling surface, using ½" or ⅝" wallboard, then finish the outside corners of the box with corner bead **(photo 2)**. Tape and finish the vertical inside corners of the boxes, as well as both horizontal inside corners along the short ends. Paint the entire surface inside each box with a light-colored, semi-gloss latex paint.

Install the fixtures in each box, positioning them so that the lamp will face the center of the box. Center the fixtures from side to side, and fasten them to the joists with screws **(photo 3)**. Connect the fixture wiring to the circuit cables, following the manufacturer's instructions.

Prepare & Install the Molding & Spacers

Cut the crown molding to fit snugly between the ends of the boxes. Paint the front faces of the molding, using the same paint used in the boxes. Line the inside surfaces of the molding pieces with reflective foil duct tape **(photo 4)**.

To determine the size of the spacers, position a piece of molding under a fixture with a lamp installed. Move the molding up and down, and hold it away from the wall until you find the best position. Holding the molding in that position, measure from the bottom back edge of the molding to the side of the box to determine the width of the spacer.

Cut the spacers to width from 2 × lumber, then cut the spacers the same length as the crown molding pieces **(photo 5)**. Sand out any saw

2 Install wallboard inside the boxes and on the ceiling, then finish all corners that will be exposed.

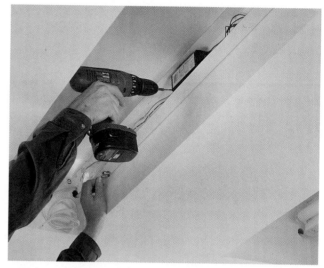

3 Attach the fixtures to the box sides (joists), then complete all of the wiring connections.

4 Cut the crown molding pieces, and paint the front faces. Apply foil tape to the back faces.

5 Cut the spacers to width, using a circular saw. Sand the edges to remove any saw marks.

144

marks, then drill pilot holes for screws through the front edge of each spacer. If the spacers are wider than 2", counterbore the pilot holes about 1" so the screws will be recessed into the spacer to gain more holding power. Position the holes so they will be covered by the molding. Paint the spacers to match the molding.

Install the spacers inside the boxes by attaching them to the box sides with wallboard screws. Make sure all spacers are level and at the same height. Attach the crown molding pieces to the front edges of the spacers with finish nails driven through pilot holes **(photo 6).** Set the nails with a nail set, and fill the holes with wood putty. Seal any gaps at the ends of the molding with paintable latex caulk, then touch-up paint the joints and nail holes.

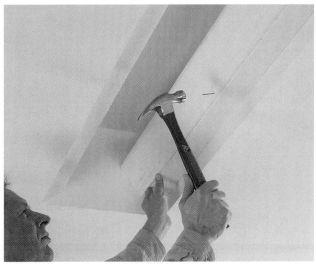

6 Position the molding pieces on the front edges of the spacers, and attach them with finish nails.

Molding Variations

With molding that's wide enough to cover the fixtures, you can omit the spacers and attach the molding directly to the box sides **(A).** You can also add molding on the ends of the boxes, fitting the pieces together with coped joints **(B).**

For a look that's more linear, use 1 × trim pieces instead of crown molding. Install nailers to the boxes, and attach the trim pieces to the nailers **(C).** This trim style looks best when the ends of the boxes are left open **(D).**

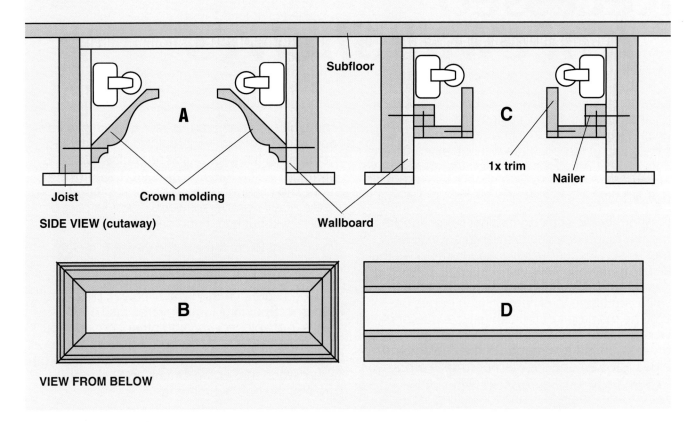

Subfloor

A

C

1x trim

Nailer

Joist   Crown molding

SIDE VIEW (cutaway)   Wallboard

B

D

VIEW FROM BELOW

Recessed Kneewall Shelves

One great way to utilize the space behind an attic kneewall is to install custom-made storage units. This recessed shelf cabinet provides over nine sq. ft. of storage area without taking up any floor space. And it's a simple project to build using standard materials and basic hand and power tools.

Support for the shelving cabinet is provided by a framed rough opening (similar to a window frame) and two pedestals made from 2 × 4s that sit below the cabinet behind the wall framing. It's best to build the rough opening and pedestals while you frame the kneewall (see pages 64-65).The main part of the cabinet is made of plywood. A face frame made of solid lumber dresses up the front edges of the cabinet and hides gaps around the wall opening. The drawings on page 147 show you all of the parts needed for the project, and the cutting list includes the materials and dimensions of each part

of the project shown.

The type of lumber you use for your shelves depends on how you want to finish them. If you'll be painting the unit, build the cabinet with A/B plywood, which has one side that's free of defects and is sanded smooth. For the face frame, use a quality-grade softwood, such as pine or aspen, without knots and saw marks.

If you want to stain the wood or apply a clear topcoat to retain the natural color, use finish-grade veneer plywood for the cabinet. Veneer plywoods are commonly available in pine, birch, and oak. Specialty lumber yards also offer veneers in maple, cherry, and other species. You can build the face frame from solid lumber that's the same species as the veneer, or choose a different wood that complements the color and grain of the cabinet material.

Everything You Need:

Tools: Circular saw, 2-ft. level, drill, framing square, bar clamps, nail set.

Materials: 2 × 4 lumber; ¾" and ¼" plywood; 1 × 4 and 1 × 2 lumber; shims; 3", 2", and 1" wallboard screws; wood glue; 3" and 1½" finish nails; fine-grit sandpaper; finishing materials; wood putty.

Frame the Rough Opening & Pedestals

Make the rough opening of the frame ½" wider and taller than the outside dimensions of the cabinet. For the project shown, the rough opening is 30½" wide × 30½" tall. For each side, attach one stud to the top and bottom plates of the kneewall (front view illustration). Attach the sill and header to the side studs, then cut and install cripple studs centered between the side studs. Make sure the studs are plumb and the sill and header are level. You can build your shelving unit to any size, but be sure to leave a few inches of space between the back of the cabinet and the rafters.

Measure from the subfloor to the top of the sill to determine the height of the pedestals (side view illustration). The length of the pedestals should equal the depth of the cabinet minus 4". Build the pedestals with 2 × 4s, then set them on the floor behind the wall so their outside edges are flush with the sides of the rough opening and their tops are flush with the sill. Make sure the pedestals are level, and shim underneath them, if necessary. Attach the pedestals to the subfloor with 3" wallboard screws.

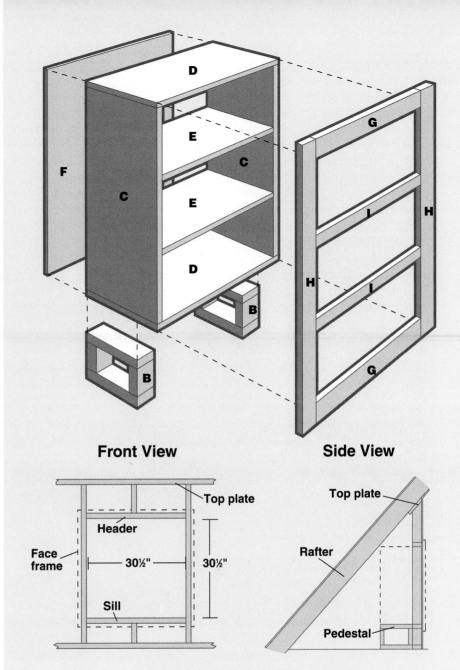

Front View

Top plate
Header
Face frame
30½"
30½"
Sill

Side View

Top plate
Rafter
Pedestal

Cutting List

Key	Part	Material	Pieces	Size
A	Header and sill	2 × 4s	1 each	30½"
B	Pedestals	2 × 4s	2	14 × 15"
C	Sides	¾" plywood	2	19 × 28½"
D	Top and bottom	¾" plywood	2	19 × 30"
E	Shelves	¾" plywood	2	19 × 28½"
F	Back panel	¼" plywood	1	30 × 30"
G	Rails	1 × 4	2	28½"
H	Stiles	1 × 4	2	35½"
I	Shelf rails	1 × 2	2	28½"

(continued next page)

Build the Cabinet

If you're building your shelves to match the project shown, cut the top, bottom, and side panels and the shelves using the dimensions shown in the cutting list on page 147 **(photo 1).** If you're custom-sizing your cabinet, measure the width and height of the rough opening, and cut the side panels 2" shorter than the height of the rough opening. Cut the top and bottom panels ½" shorter than the width of the rough opening, and cut the shelves 1½" shorter than the length of the top and bottom panels. Use a framing square to make sure the shelf and panel edges are straight and square.

Measure down from the top of each side panel, and make marks to indicate the top faces of the shelves. You can space the shelves as you like, but make sure the marks are positioned identically on both side panels. Using a framing square, draw lines through the marks on the inside faces of both side panels. Draw lines on the outside faces of the panels, ⅜" below the marks, to indicate the center of the shelves for fastening. Apply wood glue to the short edges of each shelf. Position the shelves against the side panels, aligned with the layout lines, and clamp together the assembly with bar clamps. Drill pilot holes through the side panels and into the shelf

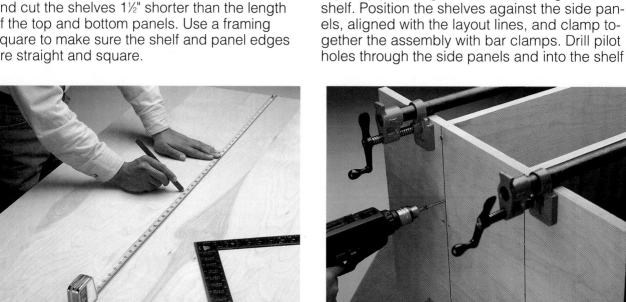

1 Cut the cabinet panels and shelves from ¾" plywood.

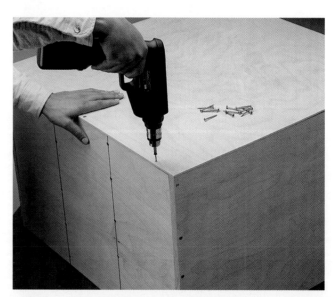

2 Draw layout lines for the shelves, then attach them between the side panels with glue and screws.

3 Fasten the top and bottom panels to the ends of the side panels.

4 Attach the back panel to the back edges of the cabinet, using screws.

edges, and fasten the pieces together with 2" wallboard screws **(photo 2).**

Fasten the top and bottom panels to the short edges of the side panels with glue and screws driven through pilot holes **(photo 3).**

Cut the back panel to size from ¼" plywood. The back panel should match the outer dimensions of the cabinet. Set the back panel over the back of the cabinet so its edges are flush with the outside faces of the bottom, top, and side panels. As you fasten the back panel, adjust the cabinet as necessary so that it's flush with the edges of the back panel. This will ensure that the cabinet is square. Drill pilot holes through the back panel where it meets the edges of the top and bottom panels and the shelves. Attach the back panel with 1" wallboard screws **(photo 4).** Do not use glue to attach the back panel.

Build & Attach the Face Frame
Cut the stiles and rails to length from 1 × 4 lumber. The stiles should equal the length of the side panels plus 7". The rails and the shelf rails should equal the length of the shelves. Apply glue to the ends of the rails and shelf rails, then assemble the face frame following the drawing on page 147. Position the shelf rails so that their top edges will be flush with the top faces of the shelves. Clamp together the frame, and measure diagonally from corner to corner to make sure the frame is square. If the dimensions are equal, the frame is square. If not, apply pressure to one side of the frame until the measurements are equal. Drill pilot holes, and toenail 3" finish nails through the ends of the rails and into the stiles **(photo 5).** Let the glue dry.

Apply glue to the front edges of the cabinet. Position the face frame over the cabinet so the inside edges of the frame are flush with the side, top, and bottom panels of the cabinet. Drill pilot holes and fasten the frame to the cabinet with 1½" finish nails, driven every 8" **(photo 6).** Set the nails with a nail set.

Finish & Install the Unit
After the glue dries completely, sand the exposed surfaces of the unit with fine-grit sandpaper. Finish the unit as desired.

Set the unit into the wall and center it within the rough opening. Anchor the unit by drilling pilot holes and driving 3" finish nails through the face frame and into the wall studs, header, and sill **(photo 7).** Space the nails evenly, and set the nail heads with a nail set. Fill the nail holes with wood putty and touch up the finish as needed.

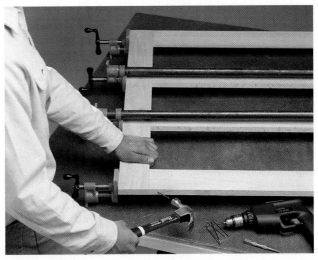

5 *Assemble the face frame pieces, and reinforce the rail-and-stile joints with toenails.*

6 *Attach the face frame to the front edges of the cabinet, using glue and finish nails.*

7 *Set the unit in place, and secure it with finish nails driven into the wall framing.*

Gas Fireplace

A new gas fireplace with direct venting can be the perfect addition to an attic or basement. Direct venting is a ventilation system that uses a special 2-in-1 vent pipe: The inner pipe carries exhaust fumes outside, while the outer pipe draws in fresh air for combustion. The vent pipe can be routed in many different ways, which means you can install a fireplace in almost any room.

Gas fireplaces are commonly available as standard *(decorative)* or *heater* types. They are similar in appearance, but heater models are designed to provide much more heat to a room. This heat can enter the room passively or be blown out by an optional electric fan. Other options for both types include remote starting and electronic ignition.

Installing a gas fireplace is a great do-it-yourself project because you can design and build the fireplace frame to suit your needs and add your own finish treatments. It all starts with some

careful planning. Once you decide on the fireplace model and determine where to place it, order all of the vent pipes and fittings needed to complete the vent run.

The project shown here includes a decorative fireplace installed in a basement. The unit is top-vented upward and out through a concrete block wall. The frame is a rectangular box that extends from floor to ceiling and is finished with wallboard. A factory-made oak mantel sits above the fireplace, and a row of ceramic floor tile surrounds the fireplace opening.

Your fireplace project can match this one, or you can adapt the basic steps to suit your own design. The main difference among fireplace installations is the venting. Regardless of your project plans, make sure to use all the required parts and follow the installation methods specified by the manufacturer and local building codes.

Planning the Project

NOTE: Consult the manufacturer's instructions for the specifications regarding placement, clearances, and venting methods for your fireplace.

Start your planning by determining the best location for the fireplace. Placing the unit next to an exterior wall simplifies the venting required. One important specification for a basement fireplace is that the *termination cap* (on the outside end of the vent) must be 12" above the ground. In the project shown, the vent runs up 3 ft. before it turns at an elbow and passes through a masonry wall. Because the wall is non-combustible, no heat shield is needed around the vent penetration.

Next, design the frame. As long as it meets the clearance requirements for your fireplace, the frame can be any size and shape you like. Typical clearance minimums include a ½" space between the framing and the sides and back of the unit and a ¼" space above the *standoffs* (for positioning and adjusting the unit). The easiest way to build a frame is to use 2 × 4s and wallboard.

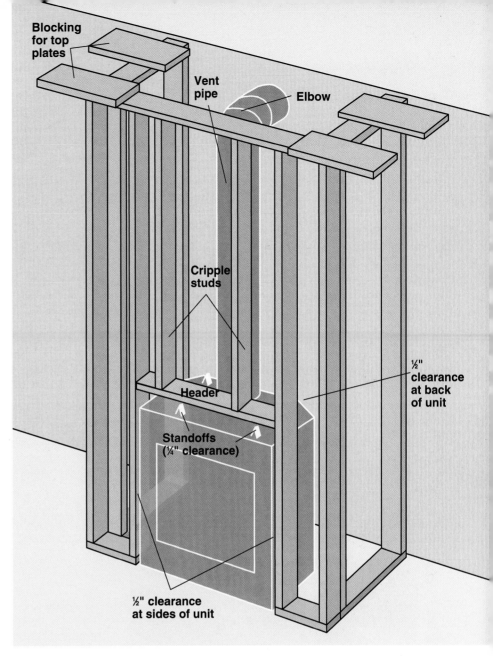

Finally, plan the rough-ins. Most fireplaces use a ½" gas supply line that connects directly to the unit. Check with the local gas utility or building department to determine what piping you'll need and the gas output required for your model. You may also need electrical wiring installed if your fireplace includes optional equipment, such as a blower or remote ignition. Complete the rough-ins after the frame is built. If you're not qualified to do the job yourself, hire professionals.

For help with any of these planning issues, talk with knowledgeable dealers in your area. They can help you choose the best fireplace model for your situation and help you with venting and other considerations. And remember, all installation specifications are governed by local building codes. Check with the building department to make sure your plans conform to regulations.

Everything You Need:

Tools: Framing square, chalk line, plumb bob, circular saw, drill, 2-ft. level, hammer drill, masonry bit, masonry chisel, hand maul, adjustable wrenches, brush, nail set, V-notched trowel, screwdriver, grout float, sponge.

Materials: Fireplace unit, vent sections, termination cap, ½" copper tubing, 2 × blocking lumber, 2 × 4 lumber, construction adhesive, masonry fasteners, 3" wallboard screws, sheet metal plates, plastic sheet, scrap plywood, sheet metal screws, caulk, ⅝" wallboard, wallboard finishing materials, high-temperature sealant, primer, paint, mantle, wood-finishing materials, 6d and 4d finish nails, wood putty, ceramic tile, tile spacers, latex tile adhesive, masking tape, grout, cap rail trim, buildup strips.

Build the Frame

Mark the outer edges of the frame onto the floor. Use a framing square to draw a perpendicular line through each mark to indicate the locations of the side walls. Measure out along these lines and mark the front of the frame, then snap a chalk line through the marks. Measure diagonally from corner to corner to make sure the layout lines are square; adjust the lines, if necessary.

Use a plumb bob to transfer the lines from the floor to the joists above. If any top plates of the frame will fall between parallel joists, install 2 × blocking between the joists. Snap a line through the marks to complete the top-plate layout.

Cut the bottom plates to size from pressure-treated 2 × 4s. Position the plates just inside the layout lines, and fasten them to the floor, using construction adhesive and masonry screws or a powder-actuated nailer (see pages 53-54). Cut the top plates from standard 2 × 4s, and attach

Header

2 *Cut and install the studs, then install the header piece to complete the front opening.*

them to the joists or blocking with 3" screws or 16d nails (drill pilot holes for screws) **(photo 1).** If the plates are attached directly to parallel joists, add backing for attaching the ceiling wallboard.

Mark the stud layout on the bottom plates, then transfer the layout to the top plates, using a plumb bob. Measure to determine the length of each stud, then cut the studs to length. Attach the two studs along the back wall using construction adhesive and masonry screws or a powder-actuated nailer. Attach the remaining studs to the top and bottom plates with 3" screws or 8d nails.

Measure up from the floor and mark the height of the header onto each stud at the side of the front opening. Cut and install the header **(photo 2).** Cut the cripple studs to fit between the header and top plate. To allow easy access for running the vent pipe, do not install the cripple studs until after the vent is in place. Add any blocking needed to provide nailing surfaces for the tile trim.

2 × blocking

1 *Draw layouts for the plates. Attach the bottom plates to the floor and the top plates to the joists.*

3 Position the fireplace inside the frame and, if necessary, install shims to bring it level.

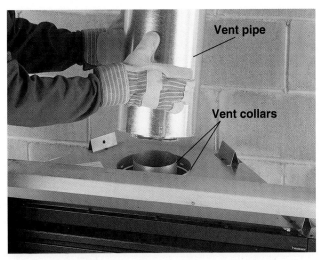

4 Dry-fit the first section of vent over the vent collars and snap it into place.

Set the Fireplace & Cut the Vent Hole

Bend out the nailing tabs at the sides of the fireplace unit. Slide the unit into the frame until the tabs meet the framing around the opening, then center the unit within the opening. Make sure the unit is level from side to side and front to back, and make any adjustments by shimming underneath with thin sheet metal plates **(photo 3).** Apply a small amount of construction adhesive to the shims to hold them in place. Measure at the sides and back of the unit to be sure the clearance requirements are met.

Dry-fit the vent pieces. Fit the flared end of the first vent section over the vent collars on top of the unit, aligning the inner and outer pipes of the vent with the matching collars **(photo 4).** Push straight down on the vent until it snaps into place over the lugs on the outside of the collar. Pull up on the vent slightly to make sure it's locked into place.

Attach the 90° elbow so that the free end points toward the exterior wall. NOTE: Horizontal vent runs must slope upward ¼" per foot. If your vent includes additional horizontal sections leading from the elbow, adjust the vent pieces and elbow to follow the required slope. Trace the circumference of the elbow end onto the wall **(photo 5).**

Remove the vent from the unit, and set it aside. Cover the fireplace with plastic and scrap plywood to protect it from debris. Using a long masonry bit and hammer drill, drill a series of holes just outside the marked circle, spacing them as close together as possible. Drill the holes all the way through the block. Be patient; the block cavities may be filled with concrete **(photo 6).**

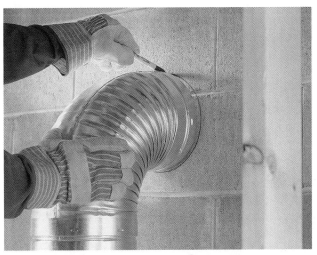

5 Mark the position of the vent hole by tracing around the circumference of the elbow.

6 Drill a series of holes through the block wall, using a hammer drill and long masonry bit.

(continued next page)

Carefully knock out the hole, using a masonry chisel and a hand maul. Work inward from both sides of the wall to ensure a clean cutout on the wall surfaces **(photo 7)**. Smooth the hole edges, test-fit the horizontal vent piece, and make any necessary adjustments. Uncover the fireplace, and clean up around the unit.

Install the Vent & Test the Fireplace

Reinstall the vertical vent section and elbow, locking the pieces together, as before. To install the adjustable horizontal vent section, measure the distance from the elbow to the termination cap. Adjust the section to length, and secure the sliding pieces together with two sheet metal screws. Install the horizontal vent section and termination cap, following the manufacturer's instructions. Seal around the perimeter of the cap with an approved caulk **(illustration)**.

When the vent run is complete, fasten the fireplace unit to the framing by driving screws through the nailing tabs. Install the cripple studs between the header and top plate.

To make the gas connection, remove the lower grill from the front of the unit. Feed the gas supply pipe into the access hole on the side of the unit, and connect it to the manual shutoff valve **(photo 8)**. Tighten the connection with adjustable wrenches.

Turn on the gas supply, and check the connection for leaking by brushing on a solution of soapy water **(photo 9)**. Bubbles indicate leaking. If you see bubbles, turn off the gas, tighten the connection, then retest it before proceeding.

Prepare the firebox, and light the fire, following the manufacturer's instructions. Let the fire run for

7 Break out the vent hole with a masonry chisel and hand maul, then carefully smooth the rough edges.

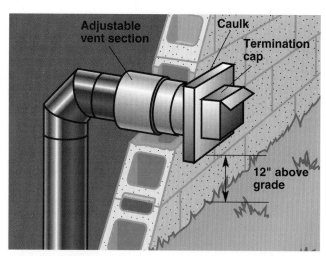

Complete the vent run by installing the adjustable vent section and termination cap. Fasten the cap to the exterior wall and seal around it with caulk.

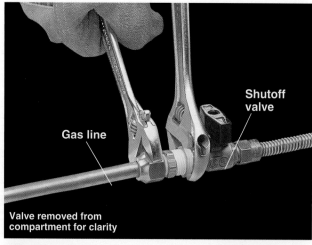

8 Connect the gas supply line to the manual shutoff valve, and carefully tighten the connection.

9 Test the gas connection for leaks by brushing on soapy water and checking for bubbles.

about 15-20 minutes while you inspect the flame and make sure there are no problems with the vent. Report any problems to the manufacturer or dealer. After the test is complete, turn off the fireplace and let it cool down completely.

Apply the Finishes

Install ⅝" wallboard over the framing, running the panels horizontally and attaching them with screws. To provide space for sealant, leave a ⅛" gap between the wallboard and the top and sides of the front face of the unit **(photo 10)**.

Fill the gap around the front face with a high-temperature sealant supplied (or recommended) by the manufacturer **(photo 11)**. Tape and finish the wallboard seams and inside corner joints, and install and finish corner bead at the outside corners. Prime and paint the areas of wallboard that

won't be covered with tile.

To install the mantle, measure up from the floor and mark the height of the support cleat. Use a level to draw a level line through the mark. Mark the stud locations just above the level line. Position the cleat on the line, centered between the frame sides, and drill a pilot hole at each stud location. Fasten the cleat to the studs with screws provided by the manufacturer **(photo 12)**.

Finish the mantle as desired, then fit it over the support cleat, and center it between the frame sides. Holding the mantle tight to the wallboard, drill pilot holes for 6d finish nails through the top of the mantle, about ¾" from the back edge. Secure the mantle to the cleat with four nails **(photo 13)**. Set the nails with a nail set, fill the holes with wood putty, then touch-up the finish.

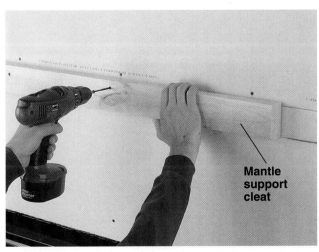

10 *Cover the frame with wallboard, leaving a gap around the black front face of the unit.*

11 *Seal around the unit's front face with high-temperature sealant.*

12 *Draw a level line for the mantle support cleat, then attach the cleat to the studs with screws.*

13 *Fit the mantle over the cleat, and secure it with finish nails driven through pilot holes.*

(continued next page)

Install the Tile & Trim

Dry-fit the tile around the front of the fireplace. You can lay tile over the black front face, but do not cover the glass or any portion of the grills. If you're using floor tile without spacer lugs on the side edges, use plastic tile spacers to set the grout gaps between tiles (at least ⅛" for floor tile). Mark the perimeter of the tile area and make any other layout marks that will help with the installation **(photo 14).** If possible, pre-cut any tiles.

Using a V-notched trowel, apply latex mastic tile adhesive to the wall, spreading it evenly just inside the perimeter lines. Set the tiles into the adhesive, aligning them with the layout marks, and press firmly to create a good bond **(photo 15).** Install spacers between tiles as you work, and scrape out excess adhesive from the grout joints, using a small screwdriver. Install all of the tile, then let the adhesive dry completely.

Mask off around the tile, then mix a batch of grout, following the manufacturer's instructions. Spread the grout over the tiles using a rubber grout float, forcing the grout into the joints **(photo 16).** Then, drag the float across the joints diagonally, tilting the float at a 45° angle Make another diagonal pass to remove excess grout. Wait 10-15 minutes, then wipe smeared grout from the tile with a damp sponge, rinsing frequently. Let the grout dry for one hour, then polish the tiles with a dry cloth. Let the grout dry completely.

Cut pieces of cap rail trim to fit around the tile, mitering the ends where the pieces fit together. If the tile is thicker than the trim recesses, install buildup strips behind the trim, using finish nails. Finish the trim to match the mantle. Drill pilot holes and nail the trim in place with 4d finish nails. Set the nails with a nail set **(photo 17).** Fill the holes with wood putty and touch up the finish.

14 *Dry-fit the tile around the fireplace front, and mark the wall to indicate tile positions.*

15 *Apply adhesive inside the layout lines, then press the tile firmly into the adhesive.*

16 *Force grout into the joints with a grout float, then make two passes to remove excess.*

17 *Attach the trim pieces around the tile with finish nails, and set the nails with a nail set.*

Credits & Additional Resources

Contributors

Airvent, Inc.
214-589-7225
www.airvent.com

Andersen Windows, Inc.
www.andersenwindows.com

Armstrong Ceilings
800-426-4261
www.armstrongceilings.com

The Bilco Company
203-934-6363
www.bilco.com

Heatway Floor Heating & Snow Melting
417-864-6108
www.heatway.com

Heatilator
800-259-1549
www.heatilator.com

Kohler Co.
800-4-KOHLER
www.kohlerco.com

Kraftmaid Cabinetry, Inc.
800-571-1990
www.kraftmaid.com

Pella Corporation
515-628-1000
www.pella.com

Pottery Barn-Kids Williams-Sonoma, Inc.
800-290-7373
www.williamssonoma.com

Room & Board
800-486-6554
www.roomandboard.com

Ultimate Electronics-AudioKing-SoundTrack
800-260-2660
www.ultimateelectronics.com

Velux-America, Inc.
800-688-3589
www.velux-america.com

Western Red Cedar Lumber Association
604-684-0266
www.wrcla.org

Photographers

Balthazar Korab, Ltd.
Troy, MI
©Balthazar Korab: pp. 17, 12

Christian Korab
Minneapolis, MN
©Christian Korab for the designer: Sarah Susanka: pp. 8, 12

Jeff Krueger
Saint Paul, MN
©Jeff Krueger for the following designers
Mulfinger, Susanka, Mahady pp. 4-5;
Sarah Susanka pp. 6-7; Mulfinger,
Susanka, Mahady, Joe Metzler p. 134;
Crystal Cabinets p. 84

Karen Melvin
Architectural Stock Images, Inc.
Minneapolis, MN
©Karen Melvin: p. 9
©Karen Melvin
for the following designers:
Portobello Designs, Inc.
Lisa Koutsky-Sten, Allied
Member ASID: p. 19;
Landschute: p. 20;
Entertainment Designs: p. 22;
Lek Design Group, Inc.: p. 23;
Vujovich Design Build: p. 27

Robert Perron
Branford, CT
©Robert Perron: pp. 13, 16, 18, 20, 21, 26, 66

Additional Resources

American Institute of Architects
800-364-9364
www.aiaonline.com

American Society of Interior Designers
202-546-3480
www.asid.org

Association of Home Appliance Manufacturers
202-872-5955
www.aham.org

National Association of the Remodeling Industry
703-575-1100
www.nari.org

National Kitchen & Bath Association (NKBA)
800-843-6522
www.nkba.com

U.S. Environmental Protection Agency
Indoor air quality
www.epa.gov/iedweb00/pubs/insidest.html

International Residential Code (book)
International Conference of Building Officials
800-284-4406
www.icbo.com

Additional Reading

from Creative Publishing international

Complete Guide to Home Carpentry
Complete Guide to Home Plumbing
Complete Guide to Home Wiring
Flooring Projects & Techniques
Complete Guide to Painting & Decorating

Creative Publishing international, Inc. offers a variety of how-to books. For information write or visit our website:
Creative Publishing international, Inc.
Subscriber Books
5900 Green Oak Drive
Minnetonka, MN 55343
www.howtobookstore.com

Metric Conversions

To Convert:	To:	Multiply by:
Inches	Millimeters	25.4
Inches	Centimeters	2.54
Feet	Meters	0.305
Yards	Meters	0.914
Square feet	Square meters	0.093
Cubic feet	Cubic meters	0.0283
Quarts (U.S.)	Liters	0.946 (Imp. 1.136)
Gallons (U.S.)	Liters	3.785 (Imp. 4.546)
Pounds	Kilograms	0.454

To Convert:	To:	Multiply by:
Millimeters	Inches	0.039
Centimeters	Inches	0.394
Meters	Feet	3.28
Meters	Yards	1.09
Square meters	Square feet	10.8
Cubic meters	Cubic feet	35.3
Liters	Quarts (U.S.)	1.057 (Imp. 0.88)
Liters	Gallons (U.S.)	0.264 (Imp. 0.22)
Kilograms	Pounds	2.2

INDEX